Barnes & Noble Shakespeare

David Scott Kastan
Series Editor

BARNES & NOBLE SHAKESPEARE features newly edited texts of the plays prepared by the world's premiere Shakespeare scholars. Each edition provides new scholarship with an introduction, commentary, unusually full and informative notes, and an essay on the history of Shakespeare's England.

DAVID SCOTT KASTAN is the George M. Bodman Professor of English at Yale University and is one of the world's leading authorities on Shakespeare.

Barnes & Noble Shakespeare
Published by Barnes & Noble
122 Fifth Avenue
New York, NY 10011
www.barnesandnoble.com/shakespeare

Image on p. 368:
William Shakespeare, *Shake-speares Sonnets*, 1609, Elizabethan Club of Yale University.

Library of Congress Cataloging-in-Publication Data

Shakespeare, William, 1564–1616.
  Sonnets / William Shakespeare ; Margreta de Grazia, editor.
    p. cm. —(Barnes & Noble Shakespeare)
  Includes bibliographical references.
  ISBN 978-1-4114-9958-4
  1. Sonnets, English. I De Grazia, Margreta. II. Title.
  PR2848.A2.D44 2011
    821'.3—dc22

                                                                2010039617

Printed and bound in the United States
1 3 5 7 9 10 8 6 4 2

SHAKESPEARE'S SONNETS

William

SHAKESPEARE

MARGRETA DE GRAZIA
EDITOR

Barnes & Noble Shakespeare

Contents

Introduction to Shakespeare's *Sonnets*
by Margreta de Grazia

ritten over four hundred years ago, Shakespeare's *Sonnets* anticipate our presence now. We are the future readers they imagine: the "eyes not yet created" which will scan their verses in time to come, the "tongues to-be" which will give them voice (Sonnet 81). Indeed the survival of the sonnets depends on our existence, for they can last only "so long as men can breathe or eyes can see" (18).

And survival into the future is the sonnets' grand aim. How else is their poet to defeat his sinister adversary? The figure of Time looms large through many of these sonnets. Though personified, its anatomy is limited to the body parts needed to wreak havoc: a cruel hand with which to grip its scythe, a swift foot with which to advance. Time moves forward like a huge threshing machine, felling everything in its path: "nothing stands but for his scythe to mow" (60). As it crushes the countryside, so too it razes the landmarks of civilization, overthrowing monuments and toppling towers. Above all, blade in hand, Time delves into the face, furrowing the brow, wrinkling the skin, leaving the visage "Beated and chopped" (62). Sometimes its strokes threaten to eradicate: "cut from memory" (63). Sometimes its deletions are gradual, as when it scrapes away inscriptions on stone or brass. Forms of writing are particularly vulnerable, as if Time took obliteration quite literally (ob-littera, to do away with letters). To counter Time, the poet writes verse. He, too, wields a cutting instrument: a pen or stylus—in origin, a sharp implement for making incisions. So armed, the poet wages war with Time, his pen against its scythe. Yet this enmity is productive: Time's decomposition precipitates the poet's composition. The sight of its wreckage impels him to write: "Ruin has taught me thus to ruminate" (64). The challenge is to capture his subject in verse before Time scythes it down. The poet bids his muse, "Give my love fame faster than time wastes life" (100). But sometimes he seems to have arrived too late: his subjects are already on the wane—faces have aged, the sun has set, summer has faded, nature is in decline.

What the poet would protect above all from Time's rampage is Beauty. Beauty in the *Sonnets* takes multiple forms, all transient and all fragile. There is "summer's honey breath" (65), youth's "rosy lips and cheeks" (116), and flowers in bloom, especially the rose. But Beauty's primary embodiment is the poet's beloved, a young man, as it turns out. The *Sonnets* open with the wish that "beauty's rose might never die," and the poet repeatedly dedicates himself to keeping the rose-like youth young and alive. He is the ideal of beauty, its map, pattern, and model; his decease would leave the world bereft. In the opening seventeen sonnets, the poet urges the young man to foil Time by replicating his image in a child. But this defense is soon superseded by an artful alternative: poetic lines take the place of genealogical lineage as a means of preserving the youth's beauty. The poet sees verse as a kind of miracle, capable of turning lifeless black into ever-living green. "His beauty shall in these black lines be seen, / And they shall live, and he in them still green" (63). He likens its magic to another sublimating process: the distillation by which the evanescent rose is preserved as lasting scent: "my verse distills your truth" (54). The second syllable of the verb "distills" holds a triple secret: Beauty is held still by poetic style fixed by the poet's stylus.

The monument is another figure for the endurance of verse: "Your monument shall be my gentle verse" (81). In the original 1609 edition, the dedication page simulates an inscribed marble slab: it is set in Roman capitals (the easiest letters to engrave on stone) with full stops separating the words (ETERNITIE and EVER-LIVING among them). The typesetting of each sonnet, when fully on the page, might also suggest a monumental form, fourteen lines of print stacked one atop the other. But the comparison of verse to a monument long pre-dates print: it derives from Ovid and Horace, great poets of the Roman Empire. As long as Roman rule lasted, as long as the Latin tongue was spoken, their poetry would endure. Unlike imperial Rome, however, Shakespeare's England was no worldwide power, his English no lingua franca. What then backs his claim to enduring fame? Nothing but the force of the poet's own imperious imperatives: "Your name from hence immortal life shall have" (81); "You still shall live" (81); "my verse shall stand" (60). The verse is self-authorizing, self-instantiating, self-empowering. And there can be no denying its efficacy. That we are still reading the sonnets, even in this very edition, is proof of their triumph over time.

Yet the victory could have gone the other way. Despite their boasts, the sonnets might have perished. Of the original edition, *Shakes-speares Sonnets*, printed in 1609, only thirteen copies (some incomplete) survive. Nor is there much evidence that the sonnets were reproduced in the writing of others. We have abundant quotations, allusions, and imitations from Shakespeare's other works throughout the seventeenth century, but few from the sonnets. Their obscurity may have something to do with the ephemeral form in which they first appeared. Unlike the plays, they never enjoyed the protection of the monumental Folio tome of 1623, *Shakespeares Comedies, Histories, & Tragedies*; had it not been for this volume, almost half of Shakespeare's plays would have been lost. His two narrative poems, *Venus and Adonis* and *Lucrece*, were also omitted, but they were so popular that, unlike the *Sonnets*, they never went out of print. Published unbound in a flimsy pamphlet consisting of a gathering of seventy-eight bio-degradable pages, the 1609 *Shake-speare's Sonnets* had more the frailty of flowers than the durability of brass. The poet hints at their perishability. Like foliage, the folios or leaves of books grow yellow with time (73); like skin, sheets of paper tan with age (17). Subject to natural decay, the sonnets might themselves have ended up rubbish, to be carried off with the "wastes of time" (12). To survive, poems likes species must reproduce: "Thou shouldst print more, not let that copy die" (11). If a copy had not surfaced in the eighteenth century and then been reprinted, *Shake-speares Sonnets* might well have died. Shakespeare's name would have survived, of course, as the author of his plays and narrative poems, but not of the sonnets.

Or not of the sonnets as we know them. For the better part of two centuries, most of them were reprinted in a volume in which they could not even be recognized as sonnets. In 1640, they appeared in a highly irregular miscellany entitled *Shakespeares Poems* where they were interspersed among poems of varying lengths and meters, many not by Shakespeare. In addition, as many as five individual sonnets were run together to form single poetic units. The fourteen-line sonnet form was lost in this scramble, and so, too, was what is now the sonnets' most prized feature: the first person, Shakespeare's "I." Many of the poems in this grab bag were narratives, ballads, and songs, delivered in the third person. Even the first-person lyrics were depersonalized or universalized by the insertion of broad generic titles that extended their applicability to any lover: "Injurious Time," "Love's Cruelty," "Beauty's Valuation."

How could the only first-person writing of the greatest author in the language ever have ended up in this jumble? Often foul play is alleged. The publisher, John Benson, is charged with having surreptitiously obtained the volume and then concealed the theft by reconfiguring the sonnets and shuffling them among poems by others. He also is accused of having altered the pronoun of Shakespeare's lover from male to female in order to avoid offending his readership. But there is an alternative explanation for Benson's innovations. In 1640, there was a demand for Shakespeare's poems, but not for his sonnets. The sonnet era of Sidney and Spenser was long gone; even in 1609 it was on the wane. The market for titillating verse, however, remained a constant. To Benson's readership, the sonnets would have appeared outmoded and monotonous. Why not enrich and enlarge the volume with different kinds of poems? The more and the more varied, the better. In addition, without a preface and with only numbers identifying each sonnet, the 1609 volume gave no discernible indication of how it should be read. The titles inserted by Benson provided each poem with a frame of reference, a context in which to be understood. With these alterations, Benson updated the volume and made it accessible. Astonishing as it may seem to modern readers, this was the form in which the sonnets circulated in the seventeenth and eighteenth centuries (in the United States, even into the nineteenth). The 1640 *Shakespeares Poems* was reprinted time and again, even in editions of Shakespeare's complete works, including the one prepared by the eighteenth century's preeminent poet, Alexander Pope.

It was not until 1780 that the sonnets were restored to their original 1609 fourteen-line form. Though the editor Edmond Malone did little to the text other than modernize spelling, he did give a clear indication of how it was to be read. The notes buttressing each sonnet highlighted the presence of the first person. So, too, they marked a partition at the irregular Sonnet 126, an envoy of six couplets to the youth. After this point, the identity (and gender) of his lover changes from fair youth to dark mistress. These two editorial prompts had an immediately stabilizing effect. The "I" was not any lover but the unique poet. The "you's" (or "thou's") were not stand-ins for any addressee: one was an individuated "he" and the other a specific "she." Footnotes strengthened the connection between Shakespeare and the first person by drawing parallels between the sonnets and Shakespeare's life, times, and other works.

Malone's identification of the sonnets' "I" with the name on the title page gave readers precisely what the plays and narrative poems had lacked: Shakespeare's own voice. The sonnets could then be read as autobiography. Scholars jumped to the conclusion that the youth to whom many of the 1609 sonnets are addressed was the same as the man to whom they are dedicated, referred to only as Mr. W.H. The most likely fit for the initials seemed to be William Herbert, Earl of Pembroke, to whom the collected plays were dedicated. If inverted, however, the initials also matched those of the dedicatee of his two narrative poems, Henry Wriothesley, Earl of Southampton. It should be noted, however, though it rarely is, that addressing either peer, in print or person, with the leveling title "Mr." would have been odd if not downright insulting.

Finding any record of a dark and promiscuous mistress has been more difficult, especially one with the musical talent implied by her provocative playing of the virginal in Sonnet 128. There is only one woman who is documented as having had relations with Shakespeare, his wife Anne; and while no wife is mentioned in the sonnets, commentators dragged her into the picture by alleging that her infidelity must have driven her husband to adultery. Such suspicions triggered the pun on her maiden name "Hathaway" in the contorted couplet of Sonnet 145, "'I hate' from hate away she threw / And saved my life, saying 'not you.'" And in the golden age of verse, there was no dearth of candidates for the rival poet mentioned in eight sonnets (78–80 and 82–86): Spenser, Marlowe, and Jonson among them. As for signs of Shakespeare himself, references to stage fright, hard times, a bad reputation, were seen to point to particulars of his life. And then there is Sonnet 136 in which he blurts out his name, "my name is Will," though significantly not to be singled out from other men but to lose himself in one great male melting pot. "Will," in addition to being, by one estimation, the name of 22½ percent of all males in England, is in early modern slang punningly synonymous with the modern "dick."

Most readers have looked to the sonnets for a different kind of access to Shakespeare, not to the persons and events in his external life, but rather to the thoughts and feelings of his inner life. Some commentators have been so struck by their personal intimacy that they have doubted that Shakespeare ever intended them for publication. So thought William Wordsworth who, in a sonnet written in praise of the sonnet, celebrated the form for providing the key with which Shakespeare unlocked his heart. Some sonnets seem to be admitting the reader into the private "sessions of sweet silent thought" (30). In the absence of personal pronouns, a number have been read as lyrical soliloquies in which the poet reflects on such subjects as mortality, mutability, loss, desire, and conscience. Many others have served as windows into Shakespeare's emotional life, particularly as he suffers his lover's absence, but also his slights, injuries, and betrayals. Many of the poems register his hurt while attempting to exonerate the cause, sometimes rationalizing offense, sometimes taking the blame on himself, and not always without bitterness and even the desire to retaliate. In the second group, his mistress's infidelity is a given of their relationship, but it can gall just the same. The tone of the sonnets to her is often playful, yet the games have a way of turning dead serious. He lightheartedly fancies himself the keys of his mistress's keyboard, moving up and down to her fingering (128); that levity disappears, however, when in Sonnet 151 those same sexual motions are seen as his "gross body's" betrayals of his soul. So, too, he takes relish in loving his mistress's lack of beauty ("My mistress' eyes are / nothing like the sun" [130]), until it translates into a defect in his vision ("mine eyes, seeing this, say this is not" [137]). In this second group, the poet pushes ambivalence beyond its limits: he admires defects, loves the abhorrent, and credits what he knows to be false.

Reflective of the workings of the mind and heart, the sonnets have been acclaimed for introducing a new kind of subjectivity to the first person of the lyric, much as Hamlet has for inaugurating psychological character into the drama. Yet however novel and original, the sonnets are written within the strictures of a highly conventional form. Also conventional are the arguments of the first seventeen sonnets urging the fair youth to marry and replicate himself in a child. As would have been apparent to Shakespeare's literate contemporaries, the so-called procreation sonnets derive from an epistle by the great humanist scholar Erasmus on marrying and begetting children. The epistle formed the basis of a standard Tudor schoolroom exercise in which boys learned how to write by amplifying and varying the Erasmian prescripts. In effect, they were being taught to reproduce precepts that urged the reproduction of their own titles, wealth, and estates: increasing their rhetorical skills to the end of multiplying their own kind. The strongest of these arguments emphasize the consequences of not doing so. To remain single and childless is, as the poet warns his fair pupil, to be guilty of narcissism, masochism, usury, suicide, and onanism. The role of women in this reproductive process is purely functional. They are the vials or virginal wombs required for childbirth. And their courtship is decidedly a matter of duty, not passion.

At the threshold of the collection, the procreation sonnets work to direct desire toward the perpetuation of the social order. But after Sonnet 17, desire deviates from the conjugal norm. The sonnets are motivated first by love of a youth so young as to be termed "boy" and second by a love of a woman so promiscuous as to be called "the wide world's common place" (137). The names of these desires may shock: sodomy and adultery. As different as the two might seem to us, they were paired in this period as types of unsanctioned copulating. Neither form of sex led to the end of legitimate children. That the poet's two sexual partners are also each other's partners puts an additional kink in the transgression.

Of course, there are other kinds of generation besides child-birth. As the poet acknowledges, a person can live on through verse as well as through children. So perhaps it is not inappropriate to think of the 154 sonnets as so many poetic offspring. Each sonnet would then be entitled to individual attention, and indeed they usually are read singly, in both editions and anthologies. This may be the best way to appreciate Shakespeare's virtuosity, from his wielding of the sonnet form to his exploitation of the smallest verbal units. Sometimes his subject conforms perfectly to the three quatrains followed by a sum-mational couplet. In Sonnet 73, for example, each quatrain frames an image of the poet's decline—late autumn, after sunset, dying embers—and the couplet gives them purpose: to increase love in the face of loss. In others, however, his subject chafes against the 4-4-4-2 structure. In Sonnet 129, the description of lust is so violently visceral that it rips through the quatrains, until it hits the end of the last; the couplet recovers balance but only to philosophize on the inevitability of what has just been unleashed. Often the couplet takes advantage of having the final word, functioning like the Last Judgment in pro-nouncing life or death to the poet or his lovers.

In many of the sonnets, formal features either enforce or undercut content. In Sonnet 107, the poet supports his claim to the eternal fame of the classics by deploying Latinate terms ("prophetic," "eclipse," "augurs," "olives," "tombs"). Sonnet 119 echoes a timeworn proverb of Solomon ("There is nothing new under the sun," Ecces. 1.9) while pondering the possibility of writing anything new. The no-toriously risqué Sonnet 20 is a tour de force of verbal ambiguity in keeping with the sexual ambiguity of his "master-mistress." Metaphor can often perform a transformative magic, as when guilty tears are converted to redemptive pearls. Puns, like those on "style" or "will" mentioned above, compress related senses into a single word. None is more profound than the three-way pun on I/eye/aye which conjoins selfhood, vision, and affirmation. The poet plays on it ostentatiously when he wistfully refers to the inception of his love as the time "when first your eye I eyed" (104). He draws on it again, less happily, in the self-castigation of Sonnet 152, of his "perjured eye," those three syllables encapsulating the complex pathology of a self subverted by affirmations known to be false, perceptions known to be blind. "Eye" is also the final word of the next-to-last sonnet, in which the poet casts himself into the mythic world of Cupid in order to stage the incurability of venereal desire. The diseased poet, unable to benefit from the therapeutic well, returns instead to the source of infection: "my mistress' eye."

Recent editors have opened up still another approach to the *Sonnets* by including a long narrative poem printed at the end of the 1609 *Sonnets*, but until recently detached from them, and either classified among Shakespeare's miscellaneous poems or else rejected as spurious. Their decision to follow the 154 sonnets with "A Lover's Complaint" is based on the conviction that the 1609 Sonnets were formatted to conform to the tripartite structure of several Elizabethan sonnet collections, by Edmund Spenser, Samuel Daniel, Thomas Lodge, and others, consisting of sonnets, Cupid poems, and a complaint. Written in a self-consciously archaic style, "A Complaint" centers on a maiden's account of her seduction and abandonment. The opening lines describe her lament as an echo, as if it were resounding from the preceding sonnets. And indeed we have heard elements of the maiden's story before. Like the fair youth of the *Sonnets*, her seducer is irresistible, and to both sexes; the same schoolboy rhetoric is used to persuade the maiden to give up her maidenhead as had been used in the *Sonnets* to convince the youth to renounce his bachelorhood. Among the gifts and tokens with which her seducer woos her are recycled sonnets, though given to him rather than written by him. But it is the maiden's closing remarks that are most in keeping with the *Sonnets*. She ends her confessional narrative not lamenting her undoing but rather resolving to be undone again. Thus "A Lover's

Complaint" ends with the same recommitment to love's injury as the sonnets. In the final two Cupid sonnets, the chronically lovesick poet returns to the source of his burning venereal disease. The return to both the ancient past of Cupid and the olden days of the maiden suggests what sonnet after sonnet has demonstrated: the inexorable pull of desire.

Over the centuries, the *Sonnets* have generated a wide array of interpretative options. Editions and criticism continue to proliferate. But they live on, too, in the form of other sonnets, from the Romantic Keats to the modern Berryman, as well as in other genres, some unknown to Shakespeare, like Oscar Wilde's short-story "The Portrait of Mr W.H." or Virginia Woolf's novel *Orlando*. They have inspired musical settings, as they did in Shakespeare's time, as well as performances, both on stage and in film. Yet we still are asking, why were they written? for whom? when? in what order? The fact that these questions remain unanswered may have contributed to the sonnets' longevity, for their elusiveness has made them all the more adaptable. Shakespeare, as we have noted, predicted that his sonnets needed our "eyes" and "tongues" in order to survive (81). We might close by inverting this dependency. The fact that his sonnets have been so generative over the centuries proves that it is we who have needed them. We continue to be moved, challenged, baffled, and shocked by what can happen within the confines of a mere fourteen lines.

Shakespeare and His England
by David Scott Kastan

S hakespeare is a household name, one of those few that don't need a first name to be instantly recognized. His first name was, of course, William, and he (and it, in its Latin form, *Gulielmus*) first came to public notice on April 26, 1564, when his baptism was recorded in the parish church of Stratford-upon-Avon, a small market town about ninety miles northwest of London. It isn't known exactly when he was born, although traditionally his birthday is taken to be April 23rd. It is a convenient date (perhaps too convenient) because that was the date of his death in 1616, as well as the date of St. George's Day, the annual feast day of England's patron saint. It is possible Shakespeare was born on the 23rd; no doubt he was born within a day or two of that date. In a time of high rates of infant mortality, parents would not wait long after a baby's birth for the baptism. Twenty percent of all children would die before their first birthday.

Life in 1564, not just for infants, was conspicuously vulnerable. If one lived to age fifteen, one was likely to live into one's fifties, but probably no more than 60 percent of those born lived past their mid-teens. Whole towns could be ravaged by epidemic disease. In 1563, the year before Shakespeare was born, an outbreak of plague claimed over one third of the population of London. Fire, too, was a constant threat; the thatched roofs of many houses were highly flammable, as well as offering handy nesting places for insects and rats. Serious crop failures in several years of the decade of the 1560s created food shortages, severe enough in many cases to lead to the starvation of the elderly and the infirm, and lowering the resistances of many others so that between 1536 and 1560 influenza claimed over 200,000 lives.

Shakespeare's own family in many ways reflected these unsettling realities. He was one of eight children, two of whom did not survive their first year, one of whom died at age eight; one lived to twenty-seven, while the four surviving siblings died at ages ranging from Edmund's thirty-nine to William's own fifty-two years. William married at an unusually early age. He was only eighteen, though his wife was twenty-six, almost exactly the norm of the day for women, though men normally married also in their mid- to late twenties. Shakespeare's wife Anne was already pregnant at the time that the marriage was formally confirmed, and a daughter, Susanna, was born six months later, in May 1583. Two years later, she gave birth to twins, Hamnet and Judith. Hamnet would die in his eleventh year.

If life was always at risk from what Shakespeare would later call "the thousand natural shocks / That flesh is heir to" (*Hamlet*, 3.1.61–62), the incessant threats to peace were no less unnerving, if usually less immediately life threatening. There were almost daily rumors of foreign invasion and civil war as the Protestant Queen Elizabeth assumed the crown in 1558 upon the death of her Catholic half sister, Mary. Mary's reign had been marked by the public burnings of Protestant "heretics," by the seeming subordination of England to Spain, and by a commitment to a ruinous war with France, that, among its other effects, fueled inflation and encouraged a debasing of the currency. If, for many, Elizabeth represented the hopes for a peaceful and prosperous Protestant future, it seemed unlikely in the early days of her rule that the young monarch could hold her England together against the twin menace of the powerful Catholic monarchies of Europe and the significant part of her own population who were reluctant to give up their old faith. No wonder the Queen's principal secretary saw England in the early years of Elizabeth's rule as a land surrounded by "perils many, great and imminent."

In Stratford-upon-Avon, it might often have been easy to forget what threatened from without. The simple rural life, shared by about 90 percent of the English populace, had its reassuring natural rhythms and delights. Life was structured by the daily rising and setting of the sun, and by the change of seasons. Crops were planted and harvested; livestock was bred, its young delivered; sheep were sheared, some livestock slaughtered. Market days and fairs saw the produce and crafts of the town arrayed as people came to sell and shop—and be entertained by musicians, dancers, and troupes of actors. But even in Stratford, the lurking tensions and dangers could be daily sensed. A few months before Shakespeare was born, there had been a shocking "defacing" of images in the church, as workmen, not content merely to whitewash over the religious paintings decorating the interior as they were ordered, gouged large holes in those felt to be too "Catholic"; a few months after Shakespeare's birth, the register of the same church records another deadly outbreak of plague. The sleepy market town on the northern bank of the gently flowing river Avon was not immune from the menace of the world that surrounded it.

This was the world into which Shakespeare was born. England at his birth was still poor and backward, a fringe nation on the periphery of Europe. English itself was a minor language, hardly spoken outside of the country's borders. Religious tension was inescapable, as the traditional Catholic faith was trying determinedly to hold on, even as Protestantism was once again anxiously trying to establish itself as the national religion. The country knew itself vulnerable to serious threats both from without and from within. In 1562, the young Queen, upon whom so many people's hopes rested, almost fell victim to smallpox, and in 1569 a revolt of the Northern earls tried to remove her from power and restore Catholicism as the national religion. The following year, Pope

Pius V pronounced the excommunication of "Elizabeth, the pretended queen of England" and forbade Catholic subjects obedience to the monarch on pain of their own excommunication. "Now we are in an evil way and going to the devil," wrote one clergyman, "and have all nations in our necks."

It was a world of dearth, danger, and domestic unrest. Yet it would soon dramatically change, and Shakespeare's literary contribution would, for future generations, come to be seen as a significant measure of England's remarkable transformation. In the course of Shakespeare's life, England, hitherto an unsophisticated and underdeveloped backwater acting as a bit player in the momentous political dramas taking place on the European continent, became a confident, prosperous, global presence. But this new world was only accidentally, as it is often known today, "The Age of Shakespeare." To the degree that historical change rests in the hands of any individual, credit must be given to the Queen. This new world arguably was "The Age of Elizabeth," even if it was not the Elizabethan Golden Age, as it has often been portrayed.

The young Queen quickly imposed her personality upon the nation. She had talented councilors around her, all with strong ties to her of friendship or blood, but the direction of government was her own. She was strong willed and cautious, certain of her right to rule and convinced that stability was her greatest responsibility. The result may very well have been, as historians have often charged, that important issues facing England were never dealt with head-on and left to her successors to settle, but it meant also that she was able to keep her England unified and for the most part at peace.

Religion posed her greatest challenge, though it is important to keep in mind that in this period, as an official at Elizabeth's court said, "Religion and the commonwealth cannot be parted asunder." Faith then was not the largely voluntary commitment it is today, nor was there any idea of some separation of church and state. Religion was literally a matter of life and death, of salvation and damnation, and the Church was the Church of England. Obedience to it was not only a matter of conscience but also of law. It was the single issue on which the nation was most likely to be torn apart.

Elizabeth's great achievement was that she was successful in ensuring that the Church of England became formally a Protestant Church, but she did so without either driving most of her Catholic subjects to sedition or alienating the more radical Protestant community. The so-called "Elizabethan Settlement" forged a broad Christian community of what has been called prayer-book Protestantism, even as many of its practitioners retained, as a clergyman said, "still a smack and savor of popish principles." If there were forces on both sides who were uncomfortable with the Settlement—committed Protestants, who wanted to do away with all vestiges of the old faith, and convinced Catholics, who continued to swear their allegiance to Rome—the majority of the country, as she hoped, found ways to live comfortably both within the law and within their faith. In 1571, she wrote to the Duke of Anjou that the forms of worship she recommended would "not properly compel any man to alter his opinion in the great matters now in controversy in the Church." The official toleration of religious ambiguity, as well as the familiar experience of an official change of state religion accompanying the crowning of a new monarch, produced a world where the familiar labels of Protestant and Catholic failed to define the forms of faith that most English people practiced. But for Elizabeth, most matters of faith could be left to individuals, as long as the Church itself, and Elizabeth's position at its head, would remain unchallenged.

In international affairs, she was no less successful with her pragmatism and willingness to pursue limited goals. A complex mix of prudential concerns about religion, the economy, and national security drove her foreign policy. She did not have imperial ambitions; in the main, she wanted only to be sure there would be no invasion of England and to encourage English trade. In the event, both goals brought England into conflict with Spain, determining the increasingly anti-Catholic tendencies of English foreign policy and, almost accidentally, England's emergence as a world power. When Elizabeth came to the throne, England was in many ways a mere satellite nation to the Netherlands, which was part of the Hapsburg Empire that the Catholic Philip II (who had briefly and unhappily been married to her predecessor and half sister, Queen Mary) ruled from Spain; by the end of her reign England was Spain's most bitter rival.

The transformation of Spain from ally to enemy came in a series of small steps (or missteps), no one of which was intended to produce what in the end came to pass. A series of posturings and provocations on both sides led to the rupture. In 1568, things moved to their breaking point, as the English confiscated a large shipment of gold that the Spanish were sending to their troops in the Netherlands. The following year saw the revolt of the Catholic earls in Northern England, followed by the papal excommunication of the Queen in 1570, both of which were by many in England assumed to be at the initiative, or at very least with the tacit support, of Philip. In fact he was not involved, but England under Elizabeth would never again think of Spain as a loyal friend or reliable ally. Indeed, Spain quickly became its mortal enemy. Protestant Dutch rebels had been opposing the Spanish domination of the Netherlands since the early 1560s, but, other than periodic financial support, Elizabeth had done little to encourage them. But in 1585, she sent troops under the command of the Earl of Leicester to support the Dutch rebels against the Spanish. Philip decided then to launch a full-scale attack on England, with the aim of deposing Elizabeth and restoring the Catholic faith. An English assault on Cadiz in 1587 destroyed a number of Spanish ships, postponing Philip's plans, but in the summer of 1588 the mightiest navy in the world, Philip's grand armada, with 132 ships and 30,493 sailors and troops, sailed for England.

By all rights, it should have been a successful invasion, but a combination of questionable Spanish tactics and a fortunate shift of wind resulted in one of England's greatest victories. The English had twice failed to intercept the armada off the coast of Portugal, and the Spanish fleet made its way to England, almost catching the English ships resupplying in Plymouth. The English navy was on its heels, when conveniently the Spanish admiral decided to anchor in the English Channel off the French port of Calais to wait for additional troops coming from the Netherlands. The English attacked with fireships, sinking four Spanish galleons, and strong winds from the south prevented an effective counterattack from the Spanish. The Spanish fleet was pushed into the North Sea, where it regrouped and decided its safest course was to attempt the difficult voyage home around Scotland and Ireland, losing almost half its ships on the way. For many in England the improbable victory was a miracle, evidence of God's favor for Elizabeth and the Protestant nation. Though war with Spain would not end for another fifteen years, the victory over the armada turned England almost overnight into a major world power, buoyed by confidence that they were chosen by God and, more tangibly, by a navy that could compete for control of the seas.

From a backward and insignificant Hapsburg satellite, Elizabeth's England had become, almost by accident, the leader of Protestant Europe. But if the victory over the armada signaled England's new place in the world, it hardly marked the end of England's travails. The economy, which initially was fueled by the military buildup, in the early 1590s fell victim to inflation, heavy taxation to support the war with Spain, the inevitable wartime disruptions of trade, as well as crop failures and a general economic downturn in Europe. Ireland, over which England had been attempting to impose its rule since 1168, continued to be a source of trouble and great expense (in some years costing the crown nearly one =fifth of its total revenues). Even when the most organized of the rebellions, begun in 1594 and led by Hugh O'Neill, Earl of Tyrone, formally ended in 1603, peace and stability had not been achieved.

But perhaps the greatest instability came from the uncertainty over the succession, an uncertainty that marked Elizabeth's reign from its beginning. Her near death from smallpox in 1562 reminded the nation that an unmarried queen could not insure the succession, and Elizabeth was under constant pressure to marry and produce an heir. She was always aware of and deeply resented the pressure, announcing as early as 1559: "this shall be for me sufficient that a marble stone shall declare that a queen, having reigned such a time, lived and died a virgin." If, however, it was for her "sufficient," it was not so for her advisors and for much of the nation, who hoped she would wed. Arguably Elizabeth was the wiser, knowing that her unmarried hand was a political advantage, allowing her to diffuse threats or create alliances with the seeming possibility of a match. But as with so much in her reign, the strategy bought temporary stability at the price of longer-term solutions.

By the mid 1590s, it was clear that she would die unmarried and without an heir, and various candidates were positioning themselves to succeed her. Enough anxiety was produced that all published debate about the succession was forbidden by law. There was no direct descendant of the English crown to claim rule, and all the claimants had to reach well back into their family history to find some legitimacy. The best genealogical claim belonged to King James VI of Scotland. His mother, Mary, Queen of Scots, was the granddaughter of James IV of Scotland and Margaret Tudor, sister to Elizabeth's father, Henry VIII. Though James had right on his side, he was, it must be remembered, a foreigner. Scotland shared the island with England but was a separate nation. Great Britain, the union of England and Scotland, would not exist formally until 1707, but with Elizabeth's death early in the morning of March 24, 1603, surprisingly uneventfully the thirty-seven-year-old James succeeded to the English throne. Two nations, one king: King James VI of Scotland, King James I of England.

Most of his English subjects initially greeted the announcement of their new monarch with delight, relieved that the crown had

successfully been transferred without any major disruption and reas-
sured that the new King was married with two living sons. However,
quickly many became disenchanted with a foreign King who spoke
English with a heavy accent, and dismayed even further by the influx
of Scots in positions of power. Nonetheless, the new King's greatest
political liability may well have been less a matter of nationality than
of temperament: he had none of Elizabeth's skill and ease in publicly
wooing her subjects. The Venetian ambassador wrote back to the Doge
that the new King was unwilling to "caress the people, nor make them
that good cheer the late Queen did, whereby she won their loves."

He was aloof and largely uninterested in the daily activities
of governing, but he was interested in political theory and strongly
committed to the cause of peace. Although a steadfast Protestant, he
lacked the reflexive anti-Catholicism of many of his subjects. In England, he achieved a broadly consensual community of Protestants.
The so-called King James Bible, the famous translation published first
in 1611, was the result of a widespread desire to have an English Bible
that spoke to all the nation, transcending the religious divisions that
had placed three different translations in the hands of his subjects.
Internationally, he styled himself *Rex Pacificus* (the peace-loving king). In
1604, the Treaty of London brought Elizabeth's war with Spain formally
to an end, and over the next decade he worked to bring about political
marriages that might cement stable alliances. In 1613, he married his
daughter to the leader of the German Protestants, while the following
year he began discussions with Catholic Spain to marry his son to the
Infanta Maria. After some ten years of negotiations, James's hopes for
what was known as the Spanish match were finally abandoned, much
to the delight of the nation, whose long-felt fear and hatred for Spain
outweighed the subtle political logic behind the plan.

But if James sought stability and peace, and for the most
part succeeded in his aims (at least until 1618, when the bitter religio-
political conflicts on the European continent swirled well out of the

King's control), he never really achieved concord and cohesion. He ruled over two kingdoms that did not know, like, or even want to understand one another, and his rule did little to bring them closer together. His England remained separate from his Scotland, even as he ruled over both. And even his England remained self-divided, as in truth it always was under Elizabeth, ever more a nation of prosperity and influence but still one forged out of deep-rooted divisions of means, faiths, and allegiances that made the very nature of English identity a matter of confusion and concern. Arguably this is the very condition of great drama—sufficient peace and prosperity to support a theater industry and sufficient provocation in the troubling uncertainties about what the nation was and what fundamentally mattered to its people to inspire plays that would offer tentative solutions or at the very least make the troubling questions articulate and moving.

Nine years before James would die in 1625, Shakespeare died, having returned from London to the small market town in which he was born. If London, now a thriving modern metropolis of well over 200,000 people, had, like the nation itself, been transformed in the course of his life, the Warwickshire market town still was much the same. The house in which Shakespeare was born still stood, as did the church in which he was baptized and the school in which he learned to read and write. The river Avon still ran slowly along the town's southern limits. What had changed was that Shakespeare was now its most famous citizen, and, although it would take more than another 100 years to fully achieve this, he would in time become England's, for having turned the great ethical, social, and political issues of his own age into plays and poems that would live forever.

William Shakespeare:
A Chronology

1558	**November 17: Queen Elizabeth crowned**
1564	April 26: Shakespeare baptized, third child born to John Shakespeare and Mary Arden
1564	**May 27: Death of Jean Calvin in Geneva**
1565	John Shakespeare elected alderman in Stratford-upon-Avon
1568	**Publication of the Bishops' Bible**
1568	September 4: John Shakespeare elected Bailiff of Stratford-upon-Avon
1569	**Northern Rebellion**
1570	**Queen Elizabeth excommunicated by the Pope**
1572	**August 24: St. Bartholomew's Day Massacre in Paris**
1576	**The Theatre is built in Shoreditch**
1577–1580	**Sir Francis Drake sails around the world**
1582	November 27: Shakespeare and Anne Hathaway married (Shakespeare is 18)
1583	Queen's Men formed
1583	May 26: Shakespeare's daughter, Susanna, baptized
1584	**Failure of the Virginia Colony**

1585   February 2: Twins, Hamnet and Judith, baptized (Shakespeare is 20)

1586   **Babington Plot to dethrone Elizabeth and replace her with Mary, Queen of Scots**

1587   **February 8: Execution of Mary, Queen of Scots**

1587   **Rose Theatre built**

1588   **August: Defeat of the Spanish armada** (Shakespeare is 24)

1588   **September 4: Death of Robert Dudley, Earl of Leicester**

1590   **First three books of Spenser's *Faerie Queene* published; Marlowe's *Tamburlaine* published**

1592   March 3: *Henry VI, Part One* performed at the Rose Theatre (Shakespeare is 27)

1593   **February–November: Theaters closed because of plague**

1593   Publication of *Venus and Adonis*

1594   Publication of *Titus Andronicus*, first play by Shakespeare to appear in print (though anonymously)

1594   Lord Chamberlain's Men formed

1595   March 15: Payment made to Shakespeare, Will Kemp, and Richard Burbage for performances at court in December, 1594

1595   **Swan Theatre built**

1596   **Books 4–6 of *The Faerie Queene* published**

1596   August 11: Burial of Shakespeare's son, Hamnet (Shakespeare is 32)

1596–1599   Shakespeare living in St. Helen's, Bishopsgate, London

1596   October 20: Grant of Arms to John Shakespeare

1597	May 4: Shakespeare purchases New Place, one of the two largest houses in Stratford (Shakespeare is 33)
1598	Publication of *Love's Labor's Lost*, first extant play with Shakespeare's name on the title page
1598	Publication of Francis Meres's *Palladis Tamia*, citing Shakespeare as "the best for Comedy and Tragedy" among English writers
1599	**Opening of the Globe Theatre**
1601	**February 7: Lord Chamberlain's Men paid 40 shillings to play *Richard II* by supporters of the Earl of Essex, the day before his abortive rebellion**
1601	**February 17: Execution of Robert Devereaux, Earl of Essex**
1601	September 8: Burial of John Shakespeare
1602	May 1: Shakespeare buys 107 acres of farmland in Stratford
1603	**March 24: Queen Elizabeth dies; James VI of Scotland succeeds as James I of England** (Shakespeare is 39)
1603	May 19: Lord Chamberlain's Men reformed as the King's Men
1604	Shakespeare living with the Mountjoys, a French Huguenot family, in Cripplegate, London
1604	**First edition of Marlowe's *Dr. Faustus* published (written c. 1589)**
1604	March 15: Shakespeare named among "players" given scarlet cloth to wear at royal procession of King James
1604	Publication of authorized version of *Hamlet* (Shakespeare is 40)
1605	**Gunpowder Plot**
1605	June 5: Marriage of Susanna Shakespeare to John Hall
1608	Publication of *King Lear* (Shakespeare is 44)
1608–1609	Acquisition of indoor Blackfriars Theatre by King's Men

1609   *Sonnets* published

1611   **King James Bible published** (Shakespeare is 47)

1612   **November 6: Death of Henry, eldest son of King James**

1613   **February 14: Marriage of King James's daughter Elizabeth to Frederick, the Elector Palatine**

1613   March 10: Shakespeare, with some associates, buys gatehouse in Blackfriars, London

1613   **June 29: Fire burns the Globe Theatre**

1614   **Rebuilt Globe reopens**

1616   February 10: Marriage of Judith Shakespeare to Thomas Quiney

1616   March 25: Shakespeare's will signed

1616   April 23: Shakespeare dies (age 52)

1616   **April 23: Cervantes dies in Madrid**

1616   April 25: Shakespeare buried in Holy Trinity Church in Stratford-upon-Avon

1623   August 6: Death of Anne Shakespeare

1623   **October: Prince Charles, King James's son, returns from Madrid, having failed to arrange his marriage to Maria Anna, Infanta of Spain**

1623   First Folio published with 36 plays (18 never previously published)

Key to the *Sonnets* Text

Symbols

°   Indicates an explanation or definition in the left-hand margin.

1   Indicates a gloss on the page facing the play text.

Terms

Q   The first printing of Shakespeare's sonnets, which was published by Thomas Thorpe in 1609, and which serves as the basis of this present edition.

Sonnets

William Shakespeare

1   *From*

     See **LONGER NOTE** on page 363.

2   *beauty's rose*

     (1) beauty's high point; (2) a perfect
     example of beauty

3   *as the riper should by time decease*

     While the older (rose) inevitably
     dies

4   *bear his memory*

     I.e., remind one of his father

5   *contracted*

     (1) betrothed; (2) diminished,
     reduced. The metaphor implies
     that the youth is both enamored
     with himself and lessened by this
     self-love.

6   *Feed'st thy light's flame with self-
     substantial fuel*

     Feed yourself with your own sub-
     stance (like a burning candle)

7   *this glutton be: / To eat the world's due,
     by the grave and thee*

     Be a glutton, by consuming what
     you owe the world (i.e., children),
     and allowing the grave to do so too

1

offspring	From [1] fairest creatures we desire increase,°
So that	That° thereby beauty's rose [2] might never die,
	But as the riper should by time decease [3]
youthful; loving	His tender° heir might bear his memory. [4]
	But thou, contracted [5] to thine own bright eyes,
	Feed'st thy light's flame with self-substantial fuel, [6]
	Making a famine where abundance lies,
	Thyself thy foe, to thy sweet self too cruel.
	Thou, that art now the world's fresh ornament
radiant	And only herald to the gaudy° spring,
substance; satisfaction	Within thine own bud buriest thy content,°
fool; miser / frugality	And, tender churl,° mak'st waste in niggarding.°
	Pity the world, or else this glutton be:
	To eat the world's due, by the grave and thee. [7]

4

8

12

1   *deep trenches in thy beauty's field*

**I.e., wrinkles in your face. Time is
likened here (with *besiege* in line 1)
to a soldier digging trenches on a
battlefield.**

2   *proud livery*

**Splendid uniform, continuing the
military metaphor above**

3   *deep-sunken eyes*

**I.e., the bright eyes in line 5 of
Sonnet 1**

4   *Were an all-eating shame and thriftless
praise*

**Would be an all-consuming source
of self-recrimination and worthless
recognition**

5   *deserved thy beauty's use*

**Would this investment of your
beauty merit**

6   *Shall sum my count and make my old
excuse*

**Will settle my account (i.e., repay to
Nature the beauty I have borrowed)
and justify my old age**

7   *Proving his beauty by succession thine*

**Demonstrating he inherited his
beauty from you**

2

When forty winters shall besiege thy brow
And dig deep trenches in thy beauty's field,[1]
Thy youth's proud livery,[2] so gazed on now,

garment — Will be a tattered weed,° of small worth held.   4

Then, being asked where all thy beauty lies,

vigorous; licentious — Where all the treasure of thy lusty° days,

To say within thine own deep-sunken eyes[3]
Were an all-eating shame and thriftless praise.[4]   8
How much more praise deserved thy beauty's use[5]
If thou couldst answer, "This fair child of mine
Shall sum my count and make my old excuse,"[6]
Proving his beauty by succession thine.[7]   12

would be — This were° to be new made when thou art old,
And see thy blood warm when thou feel'st it cold.

1   *Unbless some mother*

    Deprive some woman of children

2   *thy husbandry*

    **Agricultural duties (but punning on
    the sense of marital duties)**

3   *windows of thine age*

    Your aging eyes

4   *thy golden time*

    **Your prime of youth (mirrored in
    your children)**

5   *remembered not to be*

    Only to be forgotten

3

Look in thy glass° and tell the face thou viewest, *mirror*
Now is the time that face should form another,
Whose fresh repair° if now thou not renewest *condition*
Thou dost beguile° the world, unbless some mother.[1] 4 *disappoint*
For where is she so fair whose uneared° womb *unplowed*
Disdains the tillage of thy husbandry?[2]
Or who is he so fond° will be the tomb *foolish; lovesick*
Of his self-love, to stop posterity?° 8 *future generations*
Thou art thy mother's glass,° and she in thee *image*
Calls back the lovely April of her prime;
So thou through windows of thine age[3] shalt see,
Despite° of wrinkles, this thy golden time.[4] 12 *In spite*
    But if thou live remembered not to be,[5]
    Die single and thine image dies with thee.

1   *thy beauty's legacy*

The beauty you inherited, as well as
the beauty you should bequeath to
your children

2   *bounteous largess*

I.e., abundant riches

3   *Which usèd lives th' executor to be*

Which if invested would survive
in the executor of your will
(i.e., your child)

4

Unthrifty° loveliness, why dost thou spend
Upon thyself thy beauty's legacy?[1]
Nature's bequest gives nothing, but doth lend,
And, being frank,° she lends to those are free.°
Then, beauteous niggard,° why dost thou abuse
The bounteous largess[2] given thee to give?
Profitless° usurer, why dost thou use°
So great a sum of sums yet canst not live?
For having traffic° with thyself alone,
Thou of thyself thy sweet self dost deceive.°
Then how when nature calls thee to be gone,
What acceptable audit° canst thou leave?
 Thy unused° beauty must be tombed with thee,
 Which usèd lives th' executor to be.[3]

4

8

12

Wasteful

generous / generous
miser

Unsuccessful / lend

trade; dealings
cheat; deprive

accounting
not loaned for profit

1   *Those hours that with gentle work did*
    frame / The lovely gaze where every eye
    doth dwell / Will play the tyrants to the
    very same

    **Time, which tenderly formed your
    alluring face, will also cruelly
    abuse it.**

2   *And that un-fair which fairly doth excel*

    **And make ugly that which is of
    superior beauty. (*Un-fair* is used as
    a verb for "deprive of beauty," but
    also with the sense "treat unfairly")**

3   *were not summer's distillation left, / A*
    liquid prisoner pent in walls of glass

    **If the essence of summer had not
    been distilled into perfume (made
    from the flowers)**

4   *Beauty's effect with beauty were bereft*

    **Beauty's impact would be
    destroyed along with beauty
    itself**

5

form; create	Those hours that with gentle work did frame°
object	The lovely gaze° where every eye doth dwell
	Will play the tyrants to the very same [1]
	And that un-fair which fairly doth excel. [2] 4
	For never-resting time leads summer on
ruins	To hideous winter and confounds° him there,
halted	Sap checked° with frost and lusty leaves quite gone,
	Beauty o'er-snowed and bareness everywhere. 8
	Then, were not summer's distillation left,
	A liquid prisoner pent in walls of glass, [3]
	Beauty's effect with beauty were bereft, [4]
Neither / any	Nor° it nor no° remembrance what it was. 12
	But flowers distilled, though they with winter meet,
Lose	Leese° but their show; their substance still lives sweet.

1 *ere thou be distilled*

Before you leave your essence (i.e.,
before you have children)

2 *vial*

I.e., womb (with echo of perfume
vial from Sonnet 5)

3 *forbidden usury*

Lending money at interest was
legalized in England in 1571 but
continued to be stigmatized as a
predatory business practice.

4 *Which happies those that pay the willing
loan*

Which gives pleasure to those who
agree willingly to repay what they
have borrowed

5 *That's for thyself*

So it would be for you

6 *be it ten for one*

I.e., if you multiplied yourself by
having ten children

7 *living in posterity*

Living on through your offspring

8 *To be death's conquest*

To be conquered by death

6

Then let not winter's ragged° hand deface
In thee thy summer ere thou be distilled: [1]
Make sweet some vial;[2] treasure° thou some place
With beauty's treasure ere it° be self-killed.   4
That use° is not forbidden usury[3]
Which happies those that pay the willing loan;[4]
That's for thyself[5] to breed another thee,
Or ten times happier, be it ten for one.[6]   8
Ten times thyself were happier than thou art,
If ten of thine ten times refigured° thee.
Then what could death do if thou shouldst depart,
Leaving thee living in posterity?[7]   12
Be not self-willed,° for thou art much too fair
To be death's conquest[8] and make worms thine heir.

rough — Then let not winter's ragged° hand deface
make precious — Make sweet some vial;[2] treasure° thou some place
i.e., beauty — With beauty's treasure ere it° be self-killed.
loan for profit — That use° is not forbidden usury[3]
multiplied — If ten of thine ten times refigured° thee.
stubborn — Be not self-willed,° for thou art much too fair

1   *Serving with looks*

    Attending to him with their gaze

2   *having climbed the steep-up heavenly hill*

    **I.e., [the sun] having risen
    precipitously into the sky**

3   *Resembling strong youth in his middle
    age*

    **I.e., at noon appearing like a youth
    in his prime**

4   *highmost pitch*

    Highest point

5   *weary car*

    **Alludes to the chariot of Phoebus,
    the sun god, in ancient myth, now
    wearied from traveling across the
    sky as the sun readies to set**

6   *thyself out-going in thy noon*

    Coming to the end of your prime

7   *son*

    (With pun on "sun")

7

Lo, in the orient° when the gracious light°   *east / sun*
Lifts up his° burning head, each under° eye   *its / i.e., mortal*
Doth homage to his new-appearing sight,
Serving with looks[1] his sacred majesty;   4
And having climbed the steep-up heavenly hill,[2]
Resembling strong youth in his middle age,[3]
Yet mortal looks adore his beauty still,
Attending on his golden pilgrimage.   8
But when from highmost pitch,[4] with weary car,[5]
Like feeble age he reeleth from the day,
The eyes ('fore° duteous) now converted° are   *before / averted*
From his low tract° and look another way: *trajectory*   12
    So thou, thyself out-going in thy noon,[6]
    Unlooked on diest unless thou get° a son.[7]   *beget*

1   *Music to hear, why hear'st thou music*
      sadly?

      You, whose voice is music, why are
      you sad when you hear music?

2   *Or else receiv'st with pleasure thine*
      annoy?

      Or do you enjoy that which irritates
      you?

3   *confounds / In singleness the parts that*
      thou shouldst bear

      (1) Destroys, in singing alone, your
      harmonic line; (2) destroys, by
      staying single, the traits you should
      reproduce in your children; (3) fails,
      by staying single, to take on the
      responsibilities you should bear (as
      husband and father)

4   *Whose speechless song*

      I.e., The strings' song, *speechless*
      because only instrumental

5   *Thou single wilt prove none.*

      (1) Unmarried, you will produce no
      offspring; (2) being merely one,
      you will become none (in death); (3)
      alone, you live without harmony.

8

Music to hear, why hear'st thou music sadly?[1]

Delightful things Sweets° with sweets war not; joy delights in joy.

Why lov'st thou that which thou receiv'st not gladly,

Or else receiv'st with pleasure thine annoy?[2]   4

harmony; agreement If the true concord° of well-tunèd sounds,

harmonies By unions° married, do offend thine ear,

They do but sweetly chide thee, who confounds

In singleness the parts that thou shouldst bear.[3]   8

Notice Mark° how one string, sweet husband to another,

Strikes each in each by mutual ordering,

Resembling sire and child and happy mother,

Who, all in one, one pleasing note do sing,   12

   Whose speechless song,[4] being many, seeming one,

   Sings this to thee: "Thou single wilt prove none."[5]

1   *Is it for fear to wet a widow's eye / That*
      thou consum'st thyself in single life?

      **Is it fear that your death will bring
      tears to the wife you leave behind
      that makes you waste your life
      alone?**

2   *no form of thee*

      No image of yourself

3   *may keep, / By children's eyes, her
      husband's shape in mind*

      **May remember her husband's
      appearance by looking at her
      children's eyes**

4   *Look what*

      Whatever

5   *But beauty's waste hath in the world an
      end*

      **But wasted beauty disappears from
      the world**

6   *kept unused*

      Not invested

9

Is it for fear to wet a widow's eye
That thou consum'st thyself in single life?[1]
childless/happen   Ah, if thou issueless° shalt hap° to die,
widowed   The world will wail thee like a makeless° wife;   4
continually   The world will be thy widow and still° weep,
That thou no form of thee[2] hast left behind,
individual   When every private° widow well may keep,
By children's eyes, her husband's shape in mind.[3]   8
spendthrift   Look what[4] an unthrift° in the world doth spend
its   Shifts but his° place, for still the world enjoys it;
But beauty's waste hath in the world an end,[5]
And, kept unused,[6] the user so destroys it.   12
  No love toward others in that bosom sits
  That on himself such murd'rous shame commits.

1   *For shame deny that thou bear'st love to any*

Out of a sense of shame you should deny that you love anyone

2   *Who for thyself art so unprovident*

Who are so unwilling to provide for your future

3   *stick'st not*

Do not hesitate

4   *Seeking that beauteous roof to ruinate*

I.e., trying to destroy your lovely being (by refusing to have children). *Roof* functions as a synecdoche for "house," which serves here and elsewhere as a metaphor for the body, as well as for the family lineage.

5   *change thy thought, that I may change my mind*

Change your opinion (about having children) so I may change my opinion of you.

6   *fairer lodged*

More beautifully housed

7   *Make thee another self*

I.e., duplicate yourself by having a child

8   *That beauty still may live in thine or thee*

So that beauty might continue to live on in your offspring or in you

10

For shame deny that thou bear'st love to any,[1]
Who for thyself art so unprovident.[2]
Grant,° if thou wilt, thou art belov'd of many,   *I admit*
But that thou none lov'st is most evident;   4
For thou art so possessed with murd'rous hate
That 'gainst thyself thou stick'st not[3] to conspire,
Seeking that beauteous roof to ruinate[4]
Which to repair should be thy chief desire.   8
Oh, change thy thought, that I may change my mind.[5]
Shall hate be fairer lodged[6] than gentle love?
Be as thy presence° is, gracious and kind,   *appearance*
Or to thyself at least kind-hearted prove.   12
  Make thee another self[7] for love of me,
  That beauty still may live in thine or thee.[8]

1   *As fast as thou shalt wane, so fast thou*
    grow'st / In one of thine, from that which
    thou departest

    As rapidly as age diminishes you,
    just as rapidly will a child of yours
    restore that youth which you leave
    behind.

2   *youngly thou bestow'st*

    In youth you bequeath

3   *If all were minded so, the times should*
    cease, / And threescore year would make
    the world away.

    If everyone were of the same mind
    as you (with regard to childbear-
    ing), future generations would
    never arrive, and the world would
    end in sixty years (i.e., in one life
    span).

4   *Look whom she best endowed, she gave*
    the more

    Whomever nature gave the best
    qualities, she gave most generously
    (including fertility). This may refer
    to "the parable of the talents" in
    Matthew 25:29.

5   *shouldst in bounty cherish*

    Should value by being productive

6   *seal*

    Metal or stone stamp carved to
    leave an impression in wax

11

As fast as thou shalt wane, so fast thou grow'st
In one of thine, from that which thou departest;[1]
And that fresh blood° which youngly thou bestow'st[2]
Thou mayst call thine when thou from youth
    convertest.°   4
Herein° lives wisdom, beauty, and increase;
Without this,° folly, age, and cold decay.
If all were minded so, the times should cease,
And threescore year would make the world away.[3]   8
Let those whom nature hath not made for store,°
Harsh, featureless,° and rude,° barrenly perish.
Look whom she best endowed, she gave the more,[4]
Which bounteous gift thou shouldst in bounty
    cherish.[5]   12
She carved thee for her seal,[6] and meant thereby
Thou shouldst print more, not let that copy° die.

life; vigor — And that fresh blood°

turn away — convertest.°

i.e., In marriage — Herein°

i.e., marriage — Without this,°

preservation — for store,°

ugly / ill shaped — featureless,° and rude,°

model; example — that copy°

1   *sable curls*

    Black hair

2   *girded up in sheaves*

    Tied up in bundles

3   *bier*

    (1) Small cart for carrying hay or
    grain; (2) a platform for moving a
    corpse. The ambiguity suggests
    that lack of reproduction has
    converted the harvest to a funeral.

4   *question make*

    **Enquire; wonder (i.e., ask about
    how long it will last)**

5   *That thou among the wastes of time must
    go*

    **That you must also be ruined by
    time**

6   *do themselves forsake*

    **Leave their own best qualities
    behind**

7   *Save breed to brave him when he takes
    thee hence*

    **Except having children to defy time
    after you die**

12

When I do count the clock° that tells the time,　　　*clock chimes*
And see the brave° day sunk in hideous night;　　　*splendid*
When I behold the violet past prime,
And sable curls[1] all silvered o'er with white;　　　4
When lofty trees I see barren of leaves,
Which erst° from heat did canopy° the herd,　　　*once / gave shade to*
And summer's green all girded up in sheaves[2]
Borne on the bier[3] with white and bristly beard;　　　8
Then of° thy beauty do I question make,[4]　　　*about*
That thou among the wastes of time must go,[5]
Since sweets and beauties do themselves forsake,[6]
And die as fast as they see others grow,　　　12
　And nothing 'gainst Time's scythe can make defense
　Save breed to brave him when he takes thee hence.[7]

1   *Oh, that you were yourself!*

A standard expression: "I wish you
were feeling well," but also "I wish
your being was absolute and not
contingent."

2   *you are / No longer yours than you your-*
     self here live

Your identity is sustained only while
you live on earth.

3   *And your sweet semblance to some other*
     give

And bequeath your pleasing appearance to someone else (i.e.,
have a child)

4   *house*

I.e., the youth's exterior but also his
dynastic house (as in "the house of
Tudor")

5   *husbandry*

Good management; (2) tillage. Both
senses are punning on "husband"
to continue the speaker's encour-
agement that the addressee get
married.

6   *barren rage*

Fury that would destroy all life

13

Oh, that you were yourself! [1] But, love, you are
No longer yours than you yourself here live. [2]

To protect against Against° this coming end you should prepare,
And your sweet semblance to some other give. [3]   4

So should that beauty which you hold in lease

expiration / would be Find no determination;° then you were°
Yourself again after yourself's decease,

children When your sweet issue° your sweet form should bear.   8

Who lets so fair a house [4] fall to decay,
Which husbandry [5] in honor might uphold
Against the stormy gusts of winter's day
And barren rage [6] of death's eternal cold?   12

spendthrifts Oh, none but unthrifts:° dear my love you know
You had a father; let your son say so.

1 *have astronomy*

Understand astrology

2 *Nor can I fortune to brief minutes tell*

Nor can I precisely predict what
future minutes will hold

3 *By oft predict*

By frequent indications

4 *constant stars*

I.e., thine eyes

5 *I read such art / As*

I obtain such knowledge, for
example, that

6 *If from thyself to store thou wouldst
convert*

If you would turn your attention
from yourself to providing for the
future, i.e., by having children

7 *Thy end is truth's and beauty's doom and
date.*

Your death is also the death and
limit (*date*) of truth and beauty.

14

knowledge Not from the stars do I my judgment° pluck,
And yet methinks I have astronomy,[1]
But not to tell of good or evil luck,
Of plagues, of dearths, or seasons' quality;   4
Nor can I fortune to brief minutes tell,[2]
Appointing / its Pointing° to each his° thunder, rain, and wind,
Or say with princes if it shall go well
i.e., the sky By oft predict[3] that I in heaven° find;   8
But from thine eyes my knowledge I derive,
And, constant stars,[4] in them I read such art
As[5] truth and beauty shall together thrive
If from thyself to store thou wouldst convert;[6]   12
  Or else of thee this I prognosticate:
  Thy end is truth's and beauty's doom and date.[7]

1   *huge stage*

I.e., the world, echoing the familiar
metaphor, "All the world's a stage"
(see *As You Like It*, 2.7.139)

2   *in secret influence comment*

Secretly comment (by means of
astrological influence)

3   *at height decrease*

After reaching their peak immediately deteriorate

4   *wear their brave state out of memory*

Their once beautiful condition is
soon forgotten.

5   *Then the conceit of this inconstant stay*

Then the notion of this ever-
changing time on earth

6   *I engraft you new*

I renew you (i.e., in my poetry).
Plants and trees were often renewed by grafting (i.e., inserting
into the aging plant a new shoot),
but also punning on *graphein*, the
Greek verb "to write."

15

When I consider every thing that grows

Stays   Holds° in perfection but a little moment;

That this huge stage [1] presenteth nought but shows

Whereon the stars in secret influence comment;[2]   4

prosper   When I perceive that men as plants increase,°

Encouraged / halted   Cheerèd° and checked° even by the self-same sky,

Brag / vigor   Vaunt° in their youthful sap,° at height decrease [3]

And wear their brave state out of memory;[4]   8

Then the conceit of this inconstant stay [5]

Sets you, most rich in youth, before my sight,

collaborates   Where wasteful time debateth° with decay,

To change your day of youth to sullied night;   12

entirely   And, all° in war with time for love of you,

i.e., time   As he° takes from you, I engraft you new.[6]

1   *on the top of happy hours*

   In the prime of youth

2   *painted counterfeit*

   Representation in art

3   *lines of life*

   **(1) Lines of genealogical descent; (2)
   features of your children; (3) life-
   lines on a palm; (4) perhaps also
   with a pun on "loins"**

4   *Which this time's pencil or my pupil pen /
   Neither in inward worth nor outward
   fair / Can make you live yourself in eyes
   of men*

   **Which today's painters (*pencil* =
   "paintbrush") and my pen that tries
   in verse to equal their art, cannot
   re-create, neither in inner virtue
   nor outer beauty**

5   *To give away yourself keeps yourself still*

   **Giving a part of yourself (to your
   wife; to your offspring) allows you
   to be perpetuated.**

6   *drawn*

   **I.e., in the living reproduction of
   your being (rather than by the art-
   ists' efforts)**

16

why	But wherefore° do not you a mightier way
	Make war upon this bloody tyrant Time
decaying condition	And fortify yourself in your decay°
i.e., effectual	With means more blessèd° than my barren rhyme? 4
	Now stand you on the top of happy hours,[1]
unplanted	And many maiden gardens, yet unset,°
	With virtuous wish would bear your living flowers,
	Much liker than your painted counterfeit.[2] 8
renew	So should the lines of life[3] that life repair,°
	Which this time's pencil or my pupil pen
	Neither in inward worth nor outward fair
	Can make you live yourself in eyes of men.[4] 12
	To give away yourself keeps yourself still,[5]
	And you must live, drawn[6] by your own sweet skill.

1   *fresh numbers*

   Original verses

2   *of less truth than tongue*

   Less truthful than they are talkative

3   *true rights*

   **Praise that you deserve (perhaps
   also with pun on "rites")**

4   *stretchèd meter*

   **Far-fetched verse (but also with the
   literal sense of awkward or overly
   elaborate metrical pattern)**

17

Who will believe my verse in time to come

merits If it were filled with your most high deserts?°

as yet Though yet,° Heaven knows, it is but as a tomb

qualities Which hides your life and shows not half your parts.°   4

If I could write the beauty of your eyes

And in fresh numbers[1] number all your graces,

The age to come would say, "This poet lies:

Such heavenly touches ne'er touched earthly faces."   8

So should my papers, yellowed with their age,

Be scorned, like old men of less truth than tongue,[2]

excess And your true rights[3] be termed a poet's rage°

And stretchèd meter[4] of an antique song;   12

  But were some child of yours alive that time,

  You should live twice: in it and in my rhyme.

1   *lease hath all too short a date*

   Allotted term of possession is far too brief

2   *eye of heaven*

   I.e., the sun

3   *And every fair from fair sometime declines*

   And every beautiful thing deteriorates

4   *When in eternal lines to time thou grow'st*

   When in immortal verses you become a part of time (as implied by the grafting metaphor at the end of Sonnet 15)

18

Shall I compare thee to a summer's day?

mild   Thou art more lovely and more temperate:°

Rough winds do shake the darling buds of May,

And summer's lease hath all too short a date.[1]   4

Sometime too hot the eye of heaven [2] shines,

its   And often is his° gold complexion dimmed;

And every fair from fair sometime declines,[3]

robbed of ornament   By chance or nature's changing course untrimmed.°   8

But thy eternal summer shall not fade

own   Nor lose possession of that fair thou ow'st,°

Nor shall death brag thou wand'rest in his shade,

When in eternal lines to time thou grow'st.[4]   12

So long as men can breathe or eyes can see,

i.e., this poem   So long lives this,° and this gives life to thee.

1   *phoenix*

Mythical bird said to live for five
hundred years, then to consume
itself in flames and be reborn from
its own ashes

2   *in her blood*

While still young

3   *carve not*

Do not make wrinkled

4   *antique*

(1) Ancient; (2) antic or mad (as
perhaps also in Sonnet 17, line 12)

5   *untainted do allow*

Permit him to remain unspoiled

6   *For beauty's pattern to succeeding men*

So he can be an example of beauty
to future generations

7   *ever live young*

Always be young

19

claws   Devouring Time, blunt thou the lion's paws,°
     And make the earth devour her own sweet brood;
     Pluck the keen teeth from the fierce tiger's jaws,
     And burn the long-lived phoenix[1] in her blood;[2]   4
fly by   Make glad and sorry seasons as thou fleet'st,°
     And do whate'er thou wilt, swift-footed Time,
pleasures   To the wide world and all her fading sweets.°
     But I forbid thee one most heinous crime: 8
     Oh, carve not[3] with thy hours my love's fair brow,
     Nor draw no lines there with thine antique[4] pen;
passage   Him in thy course° untainted do allow[5]
     For beauty's pattern to succeeding men.[6]   12
      Yet do thy worst, old Time; despite thy wrong,
      My love shall in my verse ever live young.[7]

1   20

See Longer Note on page 363.

2   *with Nature's own hand painted*

I.e., without makeup

3   *master-mistress of my passion*

(1) The supreme ruler of my passion;
(2) the man/woman that I love

4   *Gilding the object whereupon it gazeth*

Making more beautiful those upon
whom your glance lands (as the sun
sometimes seems to make objects
golden)

5   *A man in hue, all hues in his controlling*

A man who in his appearance (*hue*
meant "form" or "appearance," as
well as "color") keeps all others in
his power (or perhaps: is capable of
appearing in any manner)

6   *for a woman*

(1) To be a woman; (2) to be enjoyed
by a woman

7   *Till Nature as she wrought thee fell
a-doting*

Until Nature, while she was making
you, became enamored with you

8   *by addition*

(1) By honoring you; (2) by adding
something

9   *By adding one thing to my purpose
nothing*

By adding *one thing* (i.e., a penis) of
no interest to me

10   *pricked thee out*

(1) Chose you; (2) equipped you with
a penis

11   *Mine be thy love, and thy love's use their
treasure*

Give me your love and let women
get the pleasure of using you
(sexually).

20 [1]

A woman's face, with Nature's own hand painted,[2]
Hast thou, the master-mistress of my passion;[3]
A woman's gentle heart, but not acquainted
deceitful   With shifting change, as is false° women's fashion;   4
wandering   An eye more bright than theirs, less false in rolling,°
Gilding the object whereupon it gazeth;[4]
A man in hue, all hues in his controlling,[5]
Which steals men's eyes and women's souls amazeth.   8
And for a woman[6] wert thou first created,
Till Nature as she wrought thee fell a-doting,[7]
deprived   And by addition[8] me of thee defeated,°
By adding one thing to my purpose nothing.[9]   12
But since she pricked thee out[10] for women's pleasure,
Mine be thy love, and thy love's use their treasure.[11]

1   *So is it not with me as with that muse*

    **My situation is different than
    that of that poet. (*Muse* is here a
    metonym for "poet.")**

2   *painted beauty*

    **One beautified with makeup (cf.,
    the face *with nature's own hand
    painted* in Sonnet 20)**

3   *Who Heaven itself for ornament doth use*

    **Who uses even sacred comparisons
    to ornament his description**

4   *And every fair with his fair doth rehearse*

    **Comparing everything beautiful
    with the beautiful person he writes
    about**

5   *a couplement of proud compare*

    An extravagant comparison

6   *in this huge rondure hems*

    **Encloses in this great sphere
    of the universe**

7   *let me, true in love, but truly write*

    **Allow me, who loves you faithfully,
    merely to tell the truth.**

8   *hearsay*

    Unverified oral reports; gossip

9   *that purpose not to sell*

    **Since I am not trying to sell any-
    thing. ("He praises who wishes to
    sell" was a common proverb.)**

21

So is it not with me as with that muse,[1]
Inspired Stirred° by a painted beauty[2] to his verse,
Who Heaven itself for ornament doth use,[3]
And every fair with his fair doth rehearse,[4]   4

Making a couplement of proud compare[5]
With sun and moon, with earth and sea's rich gems,
splendid With April's first-born flowers, and all things rare°
That Heaven's air in this huge rondure hems.[6]   8

Oh, let me, true in love, but truly write,[7]
And then believe me: my love is as fair
As any mother's child, though not so bright
i.e., stars As those gold candles° fixed in Heaven's air.   12

Let them say more that like of hearsay[8] well:
I will not praise that purpose not to sell.[9]

1   *So long as youth and thou are of one date*

   As long as you remain young

2   *time's furrows*

   Wrinkles

3   *Then look I death my days should expiate*

   Then I expect death will end my life

4   *Is but the seemly raiment*

   Is actually the appropriate covering

5   *be of thyself so wary / As I, not for myself,*
   but for thee will

   Take care of yourself for my sake,
   as I will take care of myself, not for
   me, but for you.

6   *Presume not on thy heart when mine is*
   slain

   Do not hope to reclaim your heart
   when I die.

22

My glass° shall not persuade me I am old
So long as youth and thou are of one date,[1]
But when in thee time's furrows[2] I behold,
Then look I death my days should expiate.[3]

For all that beauty that doth cover thee
Is but the seemly raiment[4] of my heart,
Which in thy breast doth live, as thine in me.
How can I then be elder than thou art?

Oh, therefore, love, be of thyself so wary
As I, not for myself, but for thee will,[5]
Bearing thy heart, which I will keep so chary°
As tender nurse her babe from faring ill.

  Presume not on thy heart when mine is slain;[6]
  Thou gav'st me thine not to give back again.

mirror — My glass°

carefully — chary°

4

8

12

1   *As an unperfect actor*

Just as an actor who does not know
his lines

2   *is put besides*

Forgets

3   *for fear of trust*

Lacking confidence

4   *The perfect ceremony of love's rite*

The memorized lines for the ritual
of love. (*Perfect* picks up *unperfect*
in line 1; *rite*, spelled "right" in Q,
suggests both "ritual" and "deserving.")

5   *dumb presagers*

Silent messengers

6   *More than that tongue that more hath*
     more expressed

More than someone, who has often
spoken more copiously

7   *To hear with eyes belongs to love's fine wit*

The ability to recognize what is felt
is the mark of love's sharp intelligence.

23

As an unperfect actor[1] on the stage,
stage fright Who with his fear° is put besides[2] his part,
filled Or some fierce thing replete° with too much rage,
Whose strength's abundance weakens his own heart;
So I, for fear of trust,[3] forget to say
The perfect ceremony of love's rite,[4]
And in mine own love's strength seem to decay,
Overloaded O'ercharged° with burden of mine own love's might.
writing Oh, let my books° be then the eloquence
And dumb presagers[5] of my speaking breast,
reward Who plead for love and look for recompense°
More than that tongue that more hath more
expressed.[6]
Oh, learn to read what silent love hath writ:
To hear with eyes belongs to love's fine wit.[7]

1   *played the*

Behaved like a

2   *in table*

On the tablet

3   *perspective it is best painter's art*

Seen from the right angle (i.e.,
"through my eyes"), it is the
painter's best work.

4   *through the painter*

(1) By means of the painter; (2)
looking through the painter (or the
painter's eyes)

5   *my bosom's shop*

I.e., my heart (*shop* = workshop)

6   *his windows glazèd*

Its windows (i.e., my heart's) sup-
plied with glass

7   *this cunning want to grace*

Lack this skill to adorn

24

Mine eye hath played the[1] painter and hath steeled° *drawn; engraved*
Thy beauty's form in table[2] of my heart;
My body is the frame wherein 'tis held,
And perspective it is best painter's art,[3]   4
For through the painter[4] must you see his skill
To find where your true image pictured lies,
Which in my bosom's shop[5] is hanging still,° *constantly*
That hath his windows glazèd[6] with thine eyes.   8
Now see what good turns eyes for eyes have done:
Mine eyes have drawn thy shape, and thine for me
Are windows to my breast, wherethrough° the sun *through which*
Delights to peep, to gaze therein on thee.   12
  Yet eyes this cunning want to grace[7] their art;
  They draw but what they see, know not the heart.

1   *Let those who are in favor with their stars*

Allow those who have good fortune

2   *fortune of such triumph bars*

Fortune keeps from such successes

3   *Unlooked for, joy in that I honor most*

**Overlooked by fortune, I delight in
what I value most (i.e., my love).**

4   *Great princes' favorites their fair leaves
spread / But as the marigold at the sun's
eye*

**Those favored by princes only
bloom, like the marigold, when
touched by the sun. (Marigolds
were thought to open when
touched by the sun.)**

5   *at a frown*

**I.e., with any sign of displeasure
from a superior**

6   *might*

**Q prints "worth," which as it fails
to rhyme seems an obvious error;
editors have suggested *might* and
"fight" as appropriate rhyming
words here.**

7   *remove nor be removed*

Leave nor be cast out

25

Let those who are in favor with their stars [1]
Of public honor and proud titles boast,
Whilst I, whom fortune of such triumph bars, [2]
Unlooked for, joy in that I honor most. [3]

petals Great princes' favorites their fair leaves° spread
But as the marigold at the sun's eye, [4]

magnificent display And in themselves their pride° lies burièd,
For at a frown [5] they in their glory die.

tireless / celebrated The painful° warrior famousèd° for might, [6]

defeated After a thousand victories once foiled,°

erased / completely Is from the book of honor razèd° quite,°
And all the rest forgot for which he toiled;

  Then happy I that love and am beloved
  Where I may not remove nor be removed. [7]

1   *vassalage*

Allegiance, a term derived from the feudal system in which a vassal (or serf) owed loyalty and service to his lord. (In this sonnet, written in the mode of a dedication, the feudal bond serves as an analogue for the lover's loyalty as well as for the system of patronage that demands similar subjection.)

2   *Thy merit hath my duty strongly knit*

Your worth has made binding the respect I owe you.

3   *To witness duty*

To demonstrate my devotion

4   *which wit so poor as mine / May make seem bare*

Which my limited skill may make (my devotion) seem meager

5   *all naked*

In Q this is printed inside parentheses, and seems, therefore, to refer to the speaker's *duty*, which is *bare* and *tattered*, needing *apparel*.

6   *fair aspect*

Favorable astrological influence

7   *puts apparel on*

Dresses up

8   *show me*

Show me to be

26

Lord of my love, to whom in vassalage[1]
Thy merit hath my duty strongly knit,[2]
message   To thee I send this written embassage°
To witness duty,[3] not to show my wit.   4
Duty so great, which wit so poor as mine
lacking   May make seem bare,[4] in wanting° words to show it,
opinion   But that I hope some good conceit° of thine
In thy soul's thought, all naked,[5] will bestow it,   8
actions   Till whatsoever star that guides my moving°
Points on me graciously with fair aspect[6]
And puts apparel on[7] my tattered loving
To show me[8] worthy of thy sweet respect.   12
    Then may I dare to boast how I do love thee;
test   Till then, not show my head where thou mayst prove°
    me.

1   *travail*

The lack of standardization in early
modern English spelling means
that *travail* ("toil") and "travel" were
not easily distinguished. Q prints
travail, which follows from *toil* in
line 1, but the sense of "travel" gets
activated with *journey* in line 3.

2   *Looking on darkness which the blind do
see*

Gazing into darkness like that which
the blind must see

3   *imaginary sight*

I.e., imaginative power

4   *her old face*

Night is imagined as an old woman.
(Latin *nox* is feminine.)

5   *For thee, and for myself*

Because of you, and on my behalf

27

Weary with toil, I haste me to my bed,
The dear repose° for limbs with travail[1] tired,
But then begins a journey in my head
To work° my mind, when body's work's expired.   4
For then my thoughts, from far° where I abide,
Intend° a zealous pilgrimage to thee,
And keep my drooping eyelids open wide,
Looking on darkness which the blind do see.[2]   8
Save° that my soul's imaginary sight[3]
Presents thy shadow° to my sightless view,
Which, like a jewel hung in ghastly° night,
Makes black night beauteous, and her old face[4] new.   12
  Lo, thus by day my limbs, by night my mind,
  For thee, and for myself,[5] no quiet find.

place of rest (line 2)
agitate; activate (line 4)
afar; far away (line 5)
Set out upon (line 6)
Except (line 9)
image (line 10)
terrifying (line 11)

1   *return in happy plight*

Return happily from the journey (depicted in Sonnet 27)

2   *But day by night and night by day oppressed*

But night oppresses day, and day oppresses night

3   *in consent shake hands*

Have made a pact

4   *The one by toil, the other to complain / How far I toil, still farther off from thee*

The day tortures me with work; the night makes me complain how far I still am from you.

5   *And dost him grace*

And beautifies him (by taking the sun's place)

6   *When sparkling stars twire not, thou gild'st the ev'n*

When stars don't twinkle, you light up the evening.

28

How can I then return in happy plight [1]
That am debarred° the benefit of rest,
When day's oppression is not eased by night,
But day by night and night by day oppressed? [2]   4
And each, though enemies to either's° reign,
Do in consent shake hands [3] to torture me,
The one by toil, the other to complain
How far I toil, still farther off from thee. [4]   8
I tell the day to please him thou art bright
And dost him grace [5] when clouds do blot the heaven.°
So° flatter I the swart-complexioned° night:
When sparkling stars twire not, thou gild'st the ev'n. [6]   12
  But day doth daily draw my sorrows longer,
  And night doth nightly make grief's length seem
    stronger.

excluded from (line 2)
each other's (line 5)
sky (line 10)
Similarly / dark (line 11)

1   *When in disgrace with fortune and men's*
    eyes

    **When I am out of favor with luck
    and peoples' opinions**

2   *Wishing me like to one more rich in*
    hope, / Featured like him, like him
    with friends possessed

    **Wishing I resembled a person with
    better prospects of success, with
    this person's good looks, and that
    person's group of friends**

3   *With what I most enjoy contented least*

    **Least satisfied with what I have the
    most of**

4   *state*

    **Emotional condition (but *state* in
    line 14 extends this to mean also
    "position in life" or "status")**

5   *For thy sweet love remembered such*
    wealth brings / That then I scorn to
    change my state with kings.

    **When I remember your love, it
    brings such wealth that I would not
    trade my situation for a king's.**

29

When in disgrace with fortune and men's eyes [1]
I all alone beweep my outcast state,

ineffective And trouble deaf Heaven with my bootless° cries,
And look upon myself and curse my fate,   4
Wishing me like to one more rich in hope,
Featured like him, like him with friends possessed, [2]

skill / range of ability Desiring this man's art° and that man's scope,°
With what I most enjoy contented least; [3]   8
Yet in these thoughts myself almost despising,

Perchance; Happily Haply° I think on thee, and then my state, [4]
Like to the lark at break of day arising
From sullen earth, sings hymns at Heaven's gate;   12
  For thy sweet love remembered such wealth brings
  That then I scorn to change my state with kings. [5]

1   *And with old woes new wail my dear*
     time's waste

     And with old sorrows bemoan anew
     the time I have wasted

2   *Then can I drown an eye, unused to flow*

     I.e., then my eyes, not prone to
     tears, begin to cry

3   *long since cancelled*

     Long ago repaid (with sadness)

4   *tell o'er*

     (1) Retell; (2) summarize

5   *account*

     (1) Tale; (2) financial reckoning

6   *the while*

     In the meantime

7   *dear friend*

     The poet, while never naming the
     addressee, refers to him as friend
     in thirteen sonnets. Friendship
     covered a range of intimacies,
     which could include sexual. The
     poet also terms his friend *sweet*
     boy **(108),** *my lovely boy* **(126), and** *my*
     love **(40).**

30

When to the sessions° of sweet silent thought   *court proceedings*
I summon up remembrance of things past,
I sigh° the lack of many a thing I sought,   *grieve for*
And with old woes new wail my dear time's waste;[1]   4
Then can I drown an eye, unused to flow,[2]
For precious friends hid in death's dateless° night,   *endless*
And weep afresh love's long since cancelled[3] woe,
And moan th' expense° of many a vanished sight.   *loss; cost*   8
Then can I grieve at grievances foregone,°   *past*
And heavily° from woe to woe tell o'er[4]   *sadly*
The sad account[5] of fore-bemoanèd° moan,   *already lamented*
Which I new pay as if not paid before.   12
  But if the while[6] I think on thee, dear friend,[7]
  All losses are restored, and sorrows end.

1   *endearèd with*

(1) Loved by; (2) made precious (more "dear") by

2   *Which I, by lacking, have supposèd dead*

That I, not being loved, presumed no longer existed

3   *And there reigns love, and all love's loving parts*

I.e., in your heart love rules, with all that accompanies it.

4   *interest of the dead, which now appear / But things removed that hidden in there lie*

Payment due to (continuing the financial metaphor of *endearèd*) the dead, who now seem merely things that have moved on from me, and now are concealed within your heart

5   *trophies of my lovers gone*

Memorials of my past lovers' victories over me

6   *Who all their parts of me to thee did give*

Who gave you all the spoils they had taken from me

7   *That due of many*

What was owed to many

8   *Their images I loved I view in thee, / And thou, all they, hast all the all of me.*

I see the images of those I have loved in you, and you, embodying all of them, now possess every part of me.

31

Thy bosom is endearèd with [1] all hearts
Which I, by lacking, have supposèd dead, [2]
And there reigns love, and all love's loving parts, [3]
And all those friends which I thought burièd. 4
mournful How many a holy and obsequious° tear
pure; faithful Hath dear religious° love stol'n from mine eye,
As interest of the dead, which now appear
But things removed that hidden in there lie. [4] 8
reside; survive Thou art the grave where buried love doth live,°
Hung with the trophies of my lovers gone, [5]
Who all their parts of me to thee did give; [6]
That due of many [7] now is thine alone. 12
Their images I loved I view in thee,
And thou, all they, hast all the all of me. [8]

1   *my well-contented day*

The day which I will welcome

2   *the bett'ring of the time*

I.e., the better poetry of this later
time

3   *Reserve them for my love, not for their
rhyme, / Exceeded by the height of
happier men*

Preserve these lines out of love for
me, not because of their literary
merit, which is excelled by men with
greater talent than mine.

4   *vouchsafe me but*

Grant me just

5   *Had my friend's muse grown with this
growing age, / A dearer birth than this his
love had brought*

If my friend's talent had matured
in this more sophisticated time, he
would have written a better poem
than this one that his love inspired.

6   *To march in ranks of better equipage*

To stand as an equal among better-
written poetry

7   *better prove*

Turn out to be superior

32

If thou survive my well-contented day [1]
When that churl Death my bones with dust shall cover,
chance / looks over And shalt by fortune° once more re-survey°
rough; uneven These poor rude° lines of thy deceasèd lover,   4
Compare them with the bett'ring of the time, [2]
excelled And, though they be outstripped° by every pen,
Reserve them for my love, not for their rhyme,
Exceeded by the height of happier men. [3]   8
Oh, then vouchsafe me but [4] this loving thought:
Had my friend's muse grown with this growing age,
A dearer birth than this his love had brought [5]
To march in ranks of better equipage. [6]   12
  But since he died, and poets better prove, [7]
  Theirs for their style I'll read, his for his love.

1   *Flatter the mountaintops with sovereign eye*

Compliment the mountains by rising to acknowledge them

2   *basest clouds*

(1) The darkest clouds; (2) those lowest in the sky

3   *my sun*

I.e., my beloved

4   *But out, alack*

But, alas

5   *Yet him for this my love no whit disdaineth.*

Yet despite this (i.e., that he can enjoy his *sun* for only *one hour*), my love takes no offense at all

6   *Suns of the world may stain when heaven's sun staineth.*

Mere mortals may be corrupted if even the sun itself can darken.

33

Full° many a glorious morning have I seen   *Very*
Flatter the mountaintops with sovereign eye,[1]
Kissing with golden face the meadows green,
Gilding° pale streams with heavenly alchemy,   *Making golden*   4
Anon° permit the basest clouds[2] to ride   *Soon*
With ugly rack° on his° celestial face,   *mass of clouds / its*
And from the forlorn world his visage hide,
Stealing unseen to west with this disgrace.°   *disfigurement; shame*   8
Ev'n so my sun[3] one early morn did shine
With all-triumphant splendor on my brow;
But out, alack,[4] he was but one hour mine;
The region° cloud hath masked him from me now.   *high*   12
  Yet him for this my love no whit disdaineth.[5]
  Suns of the world may stain when heaven's sun
    staineth.[6]

1   *rotten smoke*

     Unwholesome mist

2   *Though thou repent, yet I have still the
     loss*

     You apologize, but I still feel the
     pain.

3   *bears the strong offense's cross*

     Endures the burden of the painful
     insult. (Q prints "losse" at the end
     of the line, which most editors, as
     here, amend to *cross*, assuming (1)
     that Shakespeare did not intend to
     duplicate the word ending line 10;
     and (2) that *cross*, along with *pearl*
     and *ransom*, is part of a pattern of
     Christian imagery.)

34

Why didst thou promise such a beauteous day
And make me travel forth without my cloak,
To° let base° clouds o'ertake me in° my way,
Hiding thy brav'ry° in their rotten smoke?[1]   4
'Tis not enough that through the cloud thou break
To dry the rain on my storm-beaten face,
For no man well of such a salve can speak
That heals the wound and cures not the disgrace.°   8
Nor can thy shame give physic° to my grief;
Though thou repent, yet I have still the loss.[2]
Th' offender's sorrow lends but weak relief
To him that bears the strong offense's cross.[3]   12
  Ah, but those tears are pearl which thy love sheds,
  And they are rich, and ransom° all ill deeds.

Only to / dark / on (line 3)
splendor (line 4)
disfigurement; shame (line 8)
medicine (line 9)
atone; pay for (line 14)

97

1   *All men make faults, and even I in this, /*
     Authorizing thy trespass with compare

     Everyone makes mistakes, as I
     myself do in these words, justify-
     ing your wrongdoing with these
     comparisons.

2   *Myself corrupting, salving thy amiss*

     Compromising myself by putting a
     pretty face on your offenses

3   *Excusing thy sins more than thy sins are*

     Making excuses greater than your
     sins deserve

4   *For to thy sensual fault I bring in sense*

     Because I employ reason to forgive
     your physical, or lustful, failings

5   *Thy adverse party is thy advocate—*

     I.e., your prosecutor is the one de-
     fending you. (The diction of *adverse
     party*, *advocate*, *lawful plea*, *civil*, and
     accessory combines to produce an
     elaborate courtroom metaphor.)

6   *Such civil war is in my love and hate*

     Such a conflict in my feelings from
     my love (for you) and hate (for your
     actions)

35

longer	No more° be grieved at that which thou hast done;
	Roses have thorns, and silver fountains mud,
obscure	Clouds and eclipses stain° both moon and sun,
worm	And loathsome canker° lives in sweetest bud. 4
	All men make faults, and even I in this,
	Authorizing thy trespass with compare,[1]
	Myself corrupting, salving thy amiss,[2]
	Excusing thy sins more than thy sins are.[3] 8
	For to thy sensual fault I bring in sense—[4]
	Thy adverse party is thy advocate—[5]
	And 'gainst myself a lawful plea commence.
	Such civil war is in my love and hate[6] 12
accomplice	That I an accessory° needs must be
cruelly	To that sweet thief which sourly° robs from me.

1   *Let me confess*

This continues the themes of crime and guilt, and the assignment of blame from the previous sonnet.

2   *those blots that do with me remain /*
Without thy help by me be borne alone

Those moral failings, that are primarily mine, I will bear without your assistance.

3   *one respect*

(1) One truth; (2) a single appearance; (3) one consideration

4   *separable spite*

Painful separation

5   *though it alter not love's sole effect, /*
Yet doth it steal sweet hours from love's delight

Though it does not change the unique nature of our love, it does keep us from love's pleasure for hours.

6   *acknowledge thee, / Lest my bewailèd guilt should do thee shame*

Greet you in public, so that my own lamented guilt does not taint your reputation

7   *Unless thou take that honor from thy name*

Unless you want to lose the standing of your good name

8   *But do not so. I love thee in such sort, / As,*
thou being mine, mine is thy good report.

But do not put your reputation in jeopardy; I love you in such a way that, since you are mine, my reputation depends on yours. (Sonnet 96 ends with the same couplet.)

36

Let me confess[1] that we two must be twain,° *i.e., separated*
Although our undivided loves are one;
So shall those blots that do with me remain
Without thy help by me be borne alone.[2]   4
In our two loves there is but one respect,[3]
Though in our lives a separable spite,[4]
Which though it alter not love's sole effect,
Yet doth it steal sweet hours from love's delight.[5]   8
I may not evermore° acknowledge thee, *anymore*
Lest my bewailèd guilt should do thee shame,[6]
Nor thou with public kindness honor me,
Unless thou take that honor from thy name.[7]   12
But do not so. I love thee in such sort,
As, thou being mine, mine is thy good report.[8]

1   *made lame by fortune's dearest spite*

**Wounded by fortune's direst (*dear-
est*) malice.**

2   *Entitled in thy parts do crownèd sit*

**Have a claim to sit, crowned like
kings, among your admirable
qualities**

3   *I make my love engrafted to this store*

**I graft my love onto this host of
excellent qualities. *Engrafted* means
"attached" or "fastened," as a stalk
of a young plant might be *engrafted*
onto an older one.**

4   *Whilst that this shadow doth such
     substance give*

**While this image (of your virtues) so
nourishes me**

5   *Look what*

Whatever

6   *This wish I have, then ten times happy me*

**If I am granted this wish (of being
engrafted to your *store* of virtues),
then I will be happy ten times over.**

37

As a decrepit father takes delight
To see his active child do deeds of youth,
So I, made lame by fortune's dearest spite,[1]
from / honesty Take all my comfort of° thy worth and truth.°   4
intelligence For whether beauty, birth, or wealth, or wit,°
Or any of these all, or all, or more,
Entitled in thy parts do crownèd sit,[2]
I make my love engrafted to this store.[3]   8
So then I am not lame, poor, nor despised
Whilst that this shadow doth such substance give[4]
(of qualities); generosity That I in thy abundance° am sufficed,
And by a part of all thy glory live.   12
   Look what[5] is best, that best I wish in thee;
   This wish I have, then ten times happy me.[6]

1   *want subject to invent*

    Lack a subject to write about

2   *While thou dost breathe, that pour'st into
    my verse / Thine own sweet argument,
    too excellent / For every vulgar paper to
    rehearse*

    While you live, who provide
    yourself as the pleasing subject of
    my poetry, a topic too excellent for
    commonplace writing to discuss.

3   *Worthy perusal stand against thy sight*

    Worth reading meets your eye.

4   *give invention light*

    Ignite the creative process

5   *tenth muse*

    According to Greek myth, the
    muses were the nine daughters of
    Zeus and Mnemosyne, the goddess
    of memory, and were tradition-
    ally regarded as the source of all
    inspiration.

6   *bring forth / Eternal numbers to outlive
    long date*

    Give birth to immortal poetry that
    will outlive all temporal duration

7   *slight muse*

    Meager imagination

8   *The pain be mine, but thine shall be the
    praise*

    The imaginative effort will be mine,
    but (1) you deserve all the praise for
    inspiring me; (2) my verse will sing
    your praises.

38

How can my muse want subject to invent[1]
While thou dost breathe, that pour'st into my verse
Thine own sweet argument, too excellent
For every vulgar paper to rehearse?[2]   4
anything Oh, give thyself the thanks if aught° in me
Worthy perusal stand against thy sight,[3]
mute For who's so dumb° that cannot write to thee
When thou thyself dost give invention light?[4]   8
Be thou the tenth muse,[5] ten times more in worth
invoke Than those old nine which rhymers invocate;°
And he that calls on thee, let him bring forth
Eternal numbers to outlive long date.[6]   12
fussy If my slight muse[7] do please these curious° days,
The pain be mine, but thine shall be the praise.[8]

1   *how thy worth with manners may I sing /*
    When thou art all the better part of me

    **How can I praise your merit mod-
    estly when you are the main part
    of me?**

2   *mine own praise to mine own*

    The praise I write to my own

3   *Even for this*

    For this very reason

4   *single one*

    I.e., unity

5   *That due to thee which thou deserv'st
    alone*

    **That praise to you, which you alone
    deserve (rather than praising
    myself as well)**

6   *To entertain the time*

    Pleasantly to pass the time

7   *so sweetly dost deceive*

    **I.e., *absence* (line 9), *so sweetly*
    beguiles both *time and thoughts***

8   *that thou teachest how to make one
    twain, / By praising him here who doth
    hence remain*

    **Were it not that you teach me how
    to make a united couple, for in
    praising him in my verse he will
    always be here**

39

Oh, how thy worth with manners may I sing
When thou art all the better part of me? [1]
What can mine own praise to mine own [2] self bring,
And what is't but mine own when I praise thee?   4
Even for this, [3] let us divided live,
And our dear love lose name of single one, [4]
So that That° by this separation I may give
That due to thee which thou deserv'st alone. [5]   8
O absence, what a torment wouldst thou prove
bitter / permission Were it not thy sour° leisure gave sweet leave°
To entertain the time [6] with thoughts of love,
Which time and thoughts so sweetly dost deceive, [7]   12
  And that thou teachest how to make one twain,
  By praising him here who doth hence remain. [8]

1   *my loves*

(1) my loving feelings; (2) people I
love. This second sense implies that
the addressee has stolen a lover
from the speaker, a scenario that
is further hinted at in Sonnets 133,
134, and 144.

2   *that thou mayst true love call*

That you may rightfully call true
love

3   *All mine was thine before thou hadst this
more.*

You had all my affection and possessions before you took this extra
love.

4   *for my love*

(1) To win my love; (2) out of affection for me; (3) instead of my love;
(4) in return for my love

5   *my love receivest*

Enjoy my mistress

6   *for my love thou usest*

(1) Because you do it for love of me;
(2) for the lover you have engaged

7   *By wilful taste of what thyself refusest*

By perversely sampling what you
refuse to commit to

8   *all my poverty*

What little I have

9   *it is a greater grief / To bear love's wrong
than hate's known injury*

It hurts more to bear injuries
inflicted by a loved one, than by an
enemy.

10 *Lascivious grace, in whom all ill well
shows*

Seductive charm, in which every evil
appears good

40

Take all my loves,[1] my love; yea, take them all.
What hast thou then more than thou hadst before?
No love, my love, that thou mayst true love call.[2]
All mine was thine before thou hadst this more.[3]   4
Then if for my love[4] thou my love receivest,[5]
I cannot blame thee, for my love thou usest;[6]
But yet be blamed, if thou thyself deceivest
By wilful taste of what thyself refusest.[7]   8
I do forgive thy robb'ry, gentle thief,
for yourself   Although thou steal thee° all my poverty;[8]
And yet love knows it is a greater grief
To bear love's wrong than hate's known injury.[9]   12
  Lascivious grace, in whom all ill well shows,[10]
injuries   Kill me with spites,° yet we must not be foes.

1   *pretty wrongs*

Insignificant offenses

2   *sometime*

(1) On occasion; (2) for some time

3   *Thy beauty and thy years full well befits*

**Are wholly appropriate to your
beauty and youth**

4   *Gentle*

**(1) Tender, kind; (2) generous; (3) up-
per class (i.e., of the gentility)**

5   *what woman's son / Will sourly leave her
till he have prevailed*

**What man would ungraciously
leave her alone?**

6   *thou might'st my seat forbear*

**You might deny yourself the place
belonging to me (i.e., my mistress's
bed)**

7   *Hers, by thy beauty tempting her to
thee, / Thine, by thy beauty being false
to me*

***Her* promise to me is broken (by
your luring her away from me); *your*
promise to me is broken (by your
luring others to you).**

41

Those pretty wrongs[1] that liberty° commits   *freedom; sexual license*
When I am sometime[2] absent from thy heart,
Thy beauty and thy years full well befits,[3]
For still° temptation follows where thou art.   *continually*   4
Gentle[4] thou art, and therefore to be won;
Beauteous thou art, therefore to be assailed;°   *wooed strenuously*
And when a woman woos, what woman's son
Will sourly leave her till he have prevailed?[5]   8
Ay me, but yet thou might'st my seat forbear,[6]
And chide° thy beauty and thy straying youth,   *scold*
Who lead thee in their riot° even there   *licentiousness*
Where thou art forced to break a twofold truth:°   *promise*   12
  Hers, by thy beauty tempting her to thee,
  Thine, by thy beauty being false to me.[7]

1   *That thou hast her it is not all my grief*

**That you have her, or have had her
(sexually), is not the main source of
my sorrow**

2   *of my wailing chief*

My primary reason for sadness

3   *touches me more nearly*

Hits closer to my heart

4   *Loving offenders*

**(1) You offenders, whom I love; (2)
because I love people who offend**

5   *And for my sake even so doth she abuse me*

**And, because I love you, she does
me the wrong of loving you, too**

6   *Suff'ring my friend for my sake to approve
her*

**Allowing my friend, for my sake, to
try her out (sexually)**

7   *my love's*

I.e., my mistress's

8   *both twain*

The both of them

9   *lay on me this cross*

Place this burden on me

10   *Sweet flatt'ry!*

What a delusion!

42

That thou hast her it is not all my grief,[1]
And yet it may be said I loved her dearly;[o] *fondly; at great cost*
That she hath thee is of my wailing chief,[2]
A loss in love that touches me more nearly.[3]   4
Loving offenders,[4] thus I will excuse ye:
Thou dost love her because thou know'st I love her;
And for my sake even so doth she abuse me,[5]
Suff'ring my friend for my sake to approve her.[6]   8
If I lose thee, my loss is my love's[7] gain,
And losing her, my friend hath found that loss;
Both find each other, and I lose both twain,[8]
And both for my sake lay on me this cross.[9]   12
  But here's the joy: my friend and I are one.
  Sweet flatt'ry![10] Then she loves but me alone.

1   *And, darkly bright, are bright in dark*
    directed

    And my eyes, shining in the dark,
    are steered toward their object,
    even in the darkness

2   *whose shadow shadows doth make bright*

    Whose image (in my dreams) lights
    up the dark

3   *How would thy shadow's form form happy*
    show

    How would your actual substance
    (which lends its form to your
    shadow) make a pleasing sight

4   *To the clear day with thy much clearer*
    light, / When to unseeing eyes thy shade
    shines so

    In the light of day with your much
    clearer image, when even in
    the dark your likeness shines so
    brightly

5   *thy fair imperfect shade*

    Your beautiful but imperfect image
    (because only a dream)

6   *All days are nights to see*

    All my days are dark

43

close my eyes When most I wink,° then do mine eyes best see,
unheeded; uninteresting For all the day they view things unrespected,°
But when I sleep, in dreams they look on thee
And, darkly bright, are bright in dark directed.[1]   4
Then thou whose shadow shadows doth make
    bright,[2]
How would thy shadow's form form happy show[3]
To the clear day with thy much clearer light,
When to unseeing eyes thy shade shines so?[4]   8
How would, I say, mine eyes be blessèd made
By looking on thee in the living day,
When in dead night thy fair imperfect shade[5]
Through heavy sleep on sightless eyes doth stay?   12
  All days are nights to see[6] till I see thee,
   And nights bright days when dreams do show thee
    me.

1   *stop my way*

Get in my way

2   *despite of space*

In spite of the distance

3   *From limits far remote where thou dost stay*

From regions far away to where you are

4   *although my foot did stand*

Even if I stood

5   *As soon as think the place where he would be*

As quickly as it thinks about where it wants to be

6   *thought kills me that I am not thought*

The idea kills me that I am *dull substance* rather than thought.

7   *so much of earth and water wrought*

Since I am made of earth and water

8   *attend time's leisure*

Be time's servant (i.e., await the day when we will be reunited)

9   *heavy tears, badges of either's woe*

The *heavy tears* are signs of the sadness produced by the two elements dominating his being. The tears are *heavy* like *earth* and wet like *water*.

44

slow; heavy	If the dull° substance of my flesh were thought,
Spiteful	Injurious° distance should not stop my way; [1]
	For then, despite of space,[2] I would be brought
	From limits far remote where thou dost stay.[3]
	No matter then although my foot did stand [4]
	Upon the farthest earth removed from thee,
	For nimble thought can jump both sea and land
	As soon as think the place where he would be.[5]
	But, ah, thought kills me that I am not thought, [6]
	To leap large lengths of miles when thou art gone,
	But that, so much of earth and water wrought,[7]
	I must attend time's leisure [8] with my moan,
nothing; zero	Receiving naught° by elements so slow
Except	But° heavy tears, badges of either's woe.[9]

4

8

12

1   *The other two*

I.e., the other two elements in the human body (*air* and *fire*) in addition to the *earth* and *water* of Sonnet 44

2   *purging fire*

Suggests both the purification of metals by heating, and the Christian notion of purification of souls by the fire of the Last Judgment

3   *The first my thought, the other my desire*

The first is my *thought* (which is like *air*), the other is my *desire* (which is like *fire*).

4   *These present absent with swift motion slide*

They are at one moment present, at the next absent.

5   *In tender embassy*

As sweet messengers

6   *of four, with two alone*

of four elements, with only the two heavy ones (*earth* and *water*)

7   *oppressed with melancholy*

Utterly depressed; weighed down with sadness

8   *Until life's composition be re-cured*

Until health is restored by returning the elements to their proper proportion

9   *those swift messengers*

I.e., air and fire

10 *even but now*

Just at this moment

45

The other two,[1] slight° air and purging fire,[2]
     insubstantial

Are both with thee, wherever I abide:

The first my thought, the other my desire,[3]

These present absent with swift motion slide.[4]   4

For when these quicker° elements are gone
     swifter; livelier

In tender embassy[5] of love to thee,

My life, being made of four, with two alone[6]

Sinks down to death, oppressed with melancholy,[7]   8

Until life's composition be re-cured[8]

By those swift messengers[9] returned from thee,

Who even but now[10] come back again, assured

Of thy fair health, recounting it to me.   12

   This told, I joy; but then, no longer glad,

   I send them back again and straight° grow sad.
     abruptly

1   *the conquest of thy sight*

     The spoils of seeing you

9   *And my heart's right, thy inward love of*
     heart

     And what belongs to my heart is
     your love

2   *Mine eye my heart thy picture's sight*
     would bar

     My eye would like to prevent my
     heart from seeing your image.

3   *My heart mine eye the freedom of that*
     right

     My heart (wants to forbid) my eye
     the liberty of seeing you.

4   *thou in him dost lie*

     Your image dwells in him

5   *A closet*

     A small chest (possibly a chamber)

6   *the defendant*

     The eye is likened to a defendant
     in a trial, under prosecution by the
     heart.

7   *tenants to the heart*

     Residing in the heart (and thus
     hardly impartial)

8   *As thus: mine eye's due is thy outward*
     part

     As a result, your physical appear-
     ance is given to my eye

46

Mine eye and heart are at a mortal° war — *deadly*
How to divide the conquest of thy sight.[1]
Mine eye my heart thy picture's sight would bar;[2]
My heart mine eye the freedom of that right.[3]   4
My heart doth plead that thou in him dost lie,[4]
A closet[5] never pierced with crystal eyes,
But the defendant[6] doth that plea deny,
And says in him thy fair appearance lies.   8
To 'cide° this title° is empanellèd — *i.e., decide / i.e., case*
A quest° of thoughts, all tenants to the heart,[7] — *jury*
And by their verdict is determinèd
The clear eye's moiety° and the dear heart's part,° — *share / portion*   12
As thus: mine eye's due is thy outward part,[8]
And my heart's right, thy inward love of heart.[9]

1   *a league is took*

    An alliance is formed (after the
    mortal war of Sonnet 46)

2   *heart in love with sighs himself doth*
    smother

    When my lovesick heart smothers
    itself *with sighs*

3   *love's picture*

    I.e., painting of my love

4   *And to the painted banquet bids my heart*

    And invites my heart to celebrate
    the picture

5   *either by thy picture or my love, / Thyself*
    away are present still with me

    Even when you are away, you are
    continuously with me, either in
    your picture or in my thoughts of
    love.

6   *For thou no farther than my thoughts*
    canst move, / And I am still with them,
    and they with thee

    Since you cannot be farther away
    than my thoughts, which are
    constantly with me and which are
    constantly set on you

47

Betwixt mine eye and heart a league is took,[1]
And each doth good turns now unto the other.
When that mine eye is famished for a look,
Or heart in love with sighs himself doth smother,[2]   4
With my love's picture[3] then my eye doth feast
And to the painted banquet bids my heart.[4]
Another time mine eye is my heart's guest,
And in his thoughts of love doth share a part.   8
So, either by thy picture or my love,
Thyself away are present still with me,[5]
For thou no farther than my thoughts canst move,
And I am still with them, and they with thee;[6]   12
my thoughts   Or, if they° sleep, thy picture in my sight
Awakes my heart to heart's and eye's delight.

1   *I took my way*

    Set out on my journey

2   *Each trifle under truest bars to thrust*

    To keep every little thing under the most secure locks (*truest bars*)

3   *That to my use it might unusèd stay*

    That for my benefit it might remain untouched

4   *But thou, to whom my jewels trifles are*

    But you compared to whom my jewels are objects of little value

5   *Most worthy comfort, now my greatest grief*

    My greatest delight, now my greatest sorrow (because away from me and therefore liable to be stolen)

6   *best of dearest*

    Best among the things I value

7   *gentle closure of*

    Loving enclosure that is

8   *From whence at pleasure thou mayst come and part*

    Where you may come and go as you please

9   *For truth proves thievish for a prize so dear*

    Because even honesty can be corrupted when the treasure is so precious

48

How careful was I, when I took my way,[1]
Each trifle under truest bars to thrust,[2]
That to my use it might unusèd stay[3]
Safe from / guards From° hands of falsehood, in sure wards° of trust.   4
But thou, to whom my jewels trifles are,[4]
Most worthy comfort, now my greatest grief,[5]
Thou best of dearest,[6] and mine only care,
common Art left the prey of every vulgar° thief.   8
Thee have I not locked up in any chest,
Save where thou art not, though I feel thou art,
Within the gentle closure of[7] my breast,
From whence at pleasure thou mayst come and part;[8]   12
  And even thence thou wilt be stol'n, I fear,
  For truth proves thievish for a prize so dear.[9]

1   *Against that time*
    In preparation for that day

2   *Whenas thy love hath cast his utmost sum*
    When your love has settled its accounts

3   *advised respects*
    Well-considered motives

4   *shalt strangely pass*
    Disregard me, as if I were a stranger

5   *Shall reasons find of settled gravity*
    Shall put forward plausible arguments (against associating with me)

6   *Against that time do I ensconce me here*
    To defend against that day, I fortify myself

7   *Within the knowledge mine own desert*
    In the certainty that I get what I deserve

8   *And this my hand against myself uprear*
    (1) I raise this hand to testify against myself; (2) with this poetry (*hand* can mean "handwriting"), construct a case against myself

9   *To guard the lawful reasons on thy part*
    To protect the merits of your case

10 *To leave poor me, thou has the strength of laws*
    In leaving me, you have right on your side.

11 *Since why to love I can allege no cause*
    Since I can give no reason (1) why you should love me; (2) why I love you

49

Against that time[1] (if ever that time come)

failings When I shall see thee frown on my defects,[º]

Whenas thy love hath cast his utmost sum,[2]

Called to that audit by advised respects;[3]   4

Against that time when thou shalt strangely pass[4]

And scarcely greet me with that sun, thine eye,

When love, converted from the thing it was,

Shall reasons find of settled gravity;[5]   8

Against that time do I ensconce me here[6]

Within the knowledge of mine own desert,[7]

And this my hand against myself uprear[8]

To guard the lawful reasons on thy part.[9]   12

  To leave poor me, thou hast the strength of laws,[10]

  Since why to love I can allege no cause.[11]

1   *Doth teach that ease and that repose to say*

Teaches the comfort and rest at the end of my travel to remark

2   *The beast that bears me, tired with my woe*

The horse that carries me, wearied by the weight of my sadness

3   *made from thee*

Carried away from you

4   *My grief lies onward*

My sorrow is what I have ahead of me.

50

slowly; sadly   How heavy° do I journey on the way
    When what I seek (my weary travel's end)
    Doth teach that ease and that repose to say,[1]
    "Thus far the miles are measured from thy friend."   4
    The beast that bears me, tired with my woe,[2]
    Plods dully on to bear that weight in me,
    As if by some instinct the wretch did know
    His rider loved not speed, being made from thee.[3]   8
    The bloody spur cannot provoke him on
    That sometimes anger thrusts into his hide,
sadly   Which heavily° he answers with a groan,
painful   More sharp° to me than spurring to his side,   12
     For that same groan doth put this in my mind:
     My grief lies onward[4] and my joy behind.

1   *slow offense*

     Offense of traveling slowly

2   *my dull bearer*

     I.e., my sluggish horse (that *plods dully* in Sonnet 50)

3   *From where thou art, why should I haste me thence?*

     Why should I hurry from the place where you are?

4   *posting*

     Traveling rapidly

5   *Oh, what excuse will my poor beast then find / When swift extremity can seem but slow?*

     What excuse will my horse give, when even his fastest gallop seems slow?

6   *Then should I spur, though mounted on the wind*

     Then would I hurry, even if I were riding the wind.

7   *In wingèd speed no motion shall I know*

     Flying at such speed it still will not feel like I am moving.

8   *Shall neigh no dull flesh*

     (Desire) shall not neigh like a dull horse.

9   *love, for love*

     My love (i.e., my affection), for love's sake

10   *give him leave to go*

     (1) Allow him to go at his own speed; (2) let him go off on his own (since my desire will move faster than he can).

51

Thus can my love° excuse the slow offense [1] *affection*
Of my dull bearer,[2] when from thee I speed:° *hasten*
"From where thou art, why should I haste me thence?[3]
Till I return, of posting[4] is no need."   4
Oh, what excuse will my poor beast then find
When swift extremity can seem but slow?[5]
Then should I spur, though mounted on the wind;[6]
In wingèd speed no motion shall I know.[7]   8
Then can no horse with my desire keep pace;
Therefore desire, of perfect'st love being made,
Shall neigh no dull flesh[8] in his fiery race,
But love, for love,[9] thus shall excuse my jade:°   *old horse*   12
Since from thee going he went wilful° slow,   *deliberately*
Towards thee I'll run, and give him leave to go.[10]

1   *So am I as the rich*
    I am like a rich man.

2   *For blunting the fine point of seldom*
    pleasure
    For fear of weakening the intensity
    of a pleasure infrequently experi-
    enced

3   *Therefore are feasts so solemn and so rare*
    That is why holidays are so special
    and so uncommon

4   *seldom coming in the long year set*
    Located far apart in the long year

5   *thinly placèd*
    Sparsely distributed

6   *captain jewels in the carcanet*
    (Like) the central gems in a necklace

7   *So is the time that keeps you as my chest*
    In the same way, time is like a trea-
    sure chest that keeps you from me.

8   *To make some special instant special*
    blest / By new unfolding his imprisoned
    pride
    In order to make the moment *special*
    when its hidden splendor is
    suddenly revealed

9   *whose worthiness gives scope, / Being*
    had, to triumph; being lacked, to hope
    Whose virtues make it possible to
    rejoice in your presence, and in
    your absence to hope (that I might
    soon see you)

52

So am I as the rich¹ whose blessèd° key
i.e., bringing blessings

Can bring him to his sweet up-lockèd treasure,
The which he will not ev'ry hour survey,
For blunting the fine point of seldom pleasure.²   4
Therefore are feasts so solemn and so rare,³
Since, seldom coming in the long year set,⁴
Like stones of worth they thinly placèd⁵ are,
Or captain jewels in the carcanet.⁶   8
So is the time that keeps you as my chest,⁷
cabinet Or as the wardrobe° which the robe doth hide,
To make some special instant special blest
its By new unfolding his° imprisoned pride.⁸   12
  Blessèd are you whose worthiness gives scope,
  Being had, to triumph; being lacked, to hope.⁹

1   *your substance*

The essential matter of which you are composed

2   *That millions of strange shadows on you tend*

That countless different images follow you

3   *one shade*

One unique image

4   *And you, but one, can every shadow lend*

And you, only one person, can share your qualities with everyone else's image

5   *Describe Adonis, and the counterfeit / Is poorly imitated after you.*

Draw Adonis, or represent him in words, and you will find the image is just a poor imitation of you. (*Adonis* was a paragon of classical male beauty.)

6   *On Helen's cheek all art of beauty set, / And you in Grecian tires are painted new.*

Try to depict Helen of Troy using any form of art, and it would merely be a portrait of you in Grecian costume.

7   *The one doth shadow of your beauty show*

I.e., the spring gives an image of your beauty.

8   *The other as your bounty doth appear*

The fall harvest demonstrates your generosity.

9   *In all external grace you have some part*

In every beautiful form you have a share.

10 *you like none, none you, for constant heart*

You are like none other, and no one is like you, in the faithfulness of your heart.

53

What is your substance,[1] whereof are you made,
That millions of strange shadows on you tend?[2]
Since everyone hath, every one, one shade,[3]
And you, but one, can every shadow lend.[4]   4
Describe Adonis, and the counterfeit
Is poorly imitated after you.[5]
On Helen's cheek all art of beauty set,
And you in Grecian tires are painted new.[6]   8

harvest Speak of the spring and foison° of the year:
The one doth shadow of your beauty show,[7]
The other as your bounty doth appear,[8]

attractive / recognize And you in every blessèd° shape we know.°   12
  In all external grace you have some part,[9]
  But you like none, none you, for constant heart.[10]

1   *truth*

     Integrity; constancy

2   *The canker-blooms have full as deep a dye*

     **Scentless dog roses have just as rich
     a color**

3   *play as wantonly*

     Flutter as alluringly

4   *When summer's breath their maskèd buds
     discloses*

     **When the warm summer air reveals
     the flowers the buds have hidden**

5   *But, for their virtue only is their show, /
     They live unwooed, and unrespected fade*

     **But since their only worth lies in
     their appearance, they (i.e., the
     canker-blooms) are not coveted and
     (1) are not looked at, or (2) are not
     held in high regard**

6   *to themselves*

     alone

7   *Of their sweet deaths are sweetest odors
     made*

     **Dead roses are made into the
     sweetest perfumes.**

8   *And so of you*

     The same is true for you.

9   *that*

     I.e., your youth

10   *my verse distills your truth*

     My poetry will preserve your virtues.

54

Oh, how much more doth beauty beauteous seem

Because of By° that sweet ornament which truth [1] doth give!

lovely The rose looks fair,° but fairer we it deem

For that sweet odor which doth in it live. 4

The canker-blooms have full as deep a dye [2]

pigment As the perfumèd tincture° of the roses,

similar Hang on such° thorns, and play as wantonly, [3]

When summer's breath their maskèd buds discloses; [4] 8

But, for their virtue only is their show,

They live unwooed, and unrespected fade, [5]

Die to themselves. [6] Sweet roses do not so;

Of their sweet deaths are sweetest odors made; [7] 12

And so of you, [8] beauteous and lovely youth;

go away When that [9] shall vade,° my verse distills your truth. [10]

137

1   *the gilded monuments / Of princes*

The decorated tombs of kings

2   *these contents*

The contents of this poetry

3   *besmeared with sluttish time*

Dirtied by the messy passage of time

4   *root out the work of masonry*

Destroy all evidence of the stone-masons' labor

5   *Nor Mars his sword*

Neither the sword of Mars (the Roman god of war)

6   *living record*

Everlasting report

7   *'Gainst death and all oblivious enmity*

Opposing death and every hostile force that brings all to oblivion

8   *pace forth*

March proudly on

9   *ending doom*

Doomsday; like *judgment* in line 13, this refers to the Last Judgment, according to Christian belief the day of eternal reckoning that will end human history.

10   *that yourself arise*

When you will be resurrected

11   *dwell in lovers' eyes*

Survive in the eyes of all future lovers who will read it

55

Not marble nor the gilded monuments
Of princes[1] shall outlive this pow'rful rhyme,
But you shall shine more bright in these contents[2]
Than unswept stone besmeared with sluttish time.[3]   4

destructive When wasteful° war shall statues overturn,
battles And broils° root out the work of masonry,[4]
raging Nor Mars his sword[5] nor war's quick° fire shall burn
The living record[6] of your memory.   8

'Gainst death and all oblivious enmity[7]
Shall you pace forth;[8] your praise shall still find room
future generations Even in the eyes of all posterity°
That wear this world out to the ending doom.[9]   12

So, till the judgment that yourself arise,[10]
i.e., this poem You live in this,° and dwell in lovers' eyes.[11]

1 *Sweet love*

I.e., the *sweet* emotion of *love*

2 *Which but today by feeding is allayed, /*
Tomorrow sharpened in his former might

**Which even if it is calmed today by
feeding, returns tomorrow in its
previous intensity**

3 *So, love, be thou*

So it should be with you, love

4 *where two, contracted new, / Come daily*
to the banks, that when they see / Return
of love, more blest may be the view

**Keeping apart two newly betrothed
lovers, who come each day to the
shore, so that when their lover does
return it is even more delightful**

5 *Or call it winter, which being full of*
care, / Makes summer's welcome, thrice
more wished, more rare

**Otherwise call this interim *winter*,
which being difficult to endure,
makes the arrival of *summer* even
more eagerly anticipated and more
appreciated when it comes**

56

Sweet love,[1] renew thy force. Be it not said
hunger; sexual desire Thy edge should blunter be than appetite,°
Which but today by feeding is allayed,
Tomorrow sharpened in his former might.[2]   4
So, love, be thou,[3] although today thou fill
shut Thy hungry eyes even till they wink° with fullness,
Tomorrow see again, and do not kill
lethargy; apathy The spirit of love with a perpetual dullness.°   8
interval Let this sad int'rim° like the ocean be
separates Which parts° the shore, where two, contracted new,
Come daily to the banks, that when they see
Return of love, more blest may be the view;[4]   12
  Or call it winter, which being full of care,
  Makes summer's welcome, thrice more wished, more
    rare.[5]

1 *the hours and times of your desire*

   (1) The moments when you want me; (2) the moments when you have something for me to do

2 *no precious time at all*

   No time that is even remotely valuable

3 *chide the world-without-end hour*

   Complain about the time that seems to last forever

4 *my sovereign*

   My ruler (addressed to the young man)

5 *or your affairs suppose*

   Speculate about what you are doing

6 *those*

   I.e., the ones you are with

7 *in your will*

   With regard to your desire; but also possibly punning: "in the case of your Will (Shakespeare)"

57

Being your slave, what should I do but tend°   *attend; wait*
Upon the hours and times of your desire?[1]
I have no precious time at all[2] to spend,
Nor services to do, till you require.°   *call me*   4
Nor dare I chide the world-without-end hour[3]
Whilst I, my sovereign,[4] watch the clock for you,
Nor think the bitterness of absence sour
When you have bid your servant once adieu.   8
Nor dare I question with° my jealous thought   *motivated by*
Where you may be, or your affairs suppose,[5]
But, like a sad slave, stay and think of nought°   *nothing*
Save,° where you are, how happy you make those.[6]   *Except*   12
  So true° a fool is love that in your will,[7]   *trusting; complete*
  Though you do anything, he thinks no ill.

1 *That god*

   May that god

2 *I should in thought control*

   I should even think to regulate

3 *Or at your hand th' account of hours to*
   crave

   Or beg you to itemize the way you
   spend your time

4 *being at your beck*

   Awaiting your command

5 *Th' imprisoned absence of your liberty*

   The imprisonment that I feel when
   your freedom (i.e., licentiousness)
   takes you from me

6 *patience, tame to sufferance, bide each*
   check

   Let my *patience*, which is accus-
   tomed to misery, endure each
   insult

7 *where you list*

   Wherever you please

8 *to you it doth belong / Yourself to pardon*
   of self-doing crime

   To you belongs the responsibility
   of pardoning you for the crime you
   commit against yourself.

9 *Not blame your pleasure*

   Not criticize your desires

58

That god [1] forbid, that made me first your slave,
I should in thought control [2] your times of pleasure,
Or at your hand th' account of hours to crave, [3]

slave / wait on   Being your vassal° bound to stay° your leisure.   4

endure   Oh, let me suffer,° being at your beck, [4]
Th' imprisoned absence of your liberty; [5]
And patience, tame to sufferance, bide each check [6]
Without accusing you of injury.   8

privilege   Be where you list, [7] your charter° is so strong
authorize   That you yourself may privilege° your time
For   To° what you will; to you it doth belong
Yourself to pardon of self-doing crime. [8]   12

wait; serve   I am to wait,° though waiting so be hell,
Not blame your pleasure, [9] be it ill or well.

1   *Which, laboring for invention, bear amiss / The second burden of a former child*

    Which striving to create something new, misguidedly give birth to a child already born, i.e., produce something that already exists

2   *Since mind at first in character was done*

    From the time when human thoughts were first written down

3   *To this composèd wonder of your frame*

    In reaction to (1) the beautiful composition of your body; or (2) the beautifully composed words that describe your being

4   *Whether we are mended, or whe'er better they*

    Whether we have improved, or whether they were better than we are

5   *whether revolution be the same*

    If history's cycles keep everything the same

6   *sure I am the wits of former days / To subjects worse have given admiring praise*

    I am certain that the talented men of the past have praised inferior subjects.

59

If there be nothing new, but° that which is   *rather only*
Hath been before, how are our brains beguiled,°   *tricked*
Which, laboring for invention, bear amiss
The second burden of a former child.[1]   4
Oh, that record° could with a backward look,   *memory*
Even of five hundred courses of the sun,
Show me your image in some antique° book,   *ancient*
Since mind at first in character was done,[2]   8
That I might see what the old world could say
To this composèd wonder of your frame;[3]
Whether we are mended, or whe'er° better they,[4]   *whether*
Or whether revolution be the same.[5]   12
  Oh, sure I am the wits of former days
  To subjects worse have given admiring praise.[6]

1   *In sequent toil all forwards do contend.*

One after the other, all strive to move forward.

2   *Nativity*

(1) A newborn baby; (2) all things that are born

3   *once in the main of light*

Once it is exposed to the light of day

4   *wherewith being crowned*

Whereupon being crowned (with maturity)

5   *Crooked eclipses 'gainst his glory fight*

Malignant astrological influences assault its greatness.

6   *Time doth transfix the flourish set on youth*

Time destroys (with his *scythe*) the beautiful vitality of youth.

7   *delves the parallels*

Digs parallel trenches (i.e., creates wrinkles)

8   *Feeds on the rarities of nature's truth*

Consumes the finest specimens of nature's perfection

9   *nothing stands but for his scythe to mow*

All things that exist are destroyed by time. (Personified Time is typically armed with a scythe or sickle.)

10   *to times in hope*

Until future times only imagined

60

Like° as the waves make towards the pebbled shore,   *Just*
So do our minutes hasten to their end,
Each changing place with that which goes before.
In sequent toil all forwards do contend.[1]   4
Nativity,[2] once in the main of light,[3]
Crawls to maturity, wherewith being crowned,[4]
Crooked eclipses 'gainst his glory fight,[5]
And Time that gave doth now his gift confound.°   *destroy*   8
Time doth transfix the flourish set on youth[6]
And delves the parallels[7] in beauty's brow,
Feeds on the rarities of nature's truth,[8]
And nothing stands but for his scythe to mow.[9]   12
  And yet to times in hope[10] my verse shall stand,
  Praising thy worth, despite his° cruel hand.   *i.e., Time's*

1   *Is it thy will*

     Is it your wish that

2   *shadows like to thee*

     Images that resemble you

3   *thy spirit*

     **(1) Your inner spirit or soul; (2) your
     ghostly apparition**

4   *To find out shames and idle hours in me, /
     The scope and tenor of thy jealousy*

     **To discover my shameful behavior
     and my wasted time, legitimate
     concerns for your jealousy**

5   *my love*

     (1) My affection; (2) you, my beloved

6   *dost wake*

     **(1) Stay up late for pleasure; (2)
     wake up**

61

Is it thy will[1] thy image should keep open
My heavy eyelids to the weary night?
Dost thou desire my slumbers should be broken
delude While shadows like to thee[2] do mock° my sight?   4
Is it thy spirit[3] that thou send'st from thee
So far from home into my deeds to pry,
To find out shames and idle hours in me,
The scope and tenor of thy jealousy?[4]   8
Oh, no; thy love, though much, is not so great.
It is my love[5] that keeps mine eye awake,
Mine own true love that doth my rest defeat,
To play the watchman ever for thy sake.   12
stay awake   For thee watch° I, whilst thou dost wake[6] elsewhere,
  From me far off, with others all too near.

1 *so grounded inward*

Rooted so deeply

2 *Methinks no face so gracious is as mine*

**It seems to me no face is as beauti-
ful as my own.**

3 *No shape so true, no truth of such
account*

**No body so perfect, no perfection
of such value**

4 *for myself my own worth do define / As I
all other in all worths surmount*

**In my own words, I describe myself
so that I surpass all others in every
aspect.**

5 *shows me myself indeed*

**Reveals to me what I actually look
like**

6 *tanned antiquity*

**Weather-beaten old age (with skin
like tanned leather)**

7 *Mine own self-love quite contrary I read*

**I interpret my self-love in quite the
opposite way.**

8 *Self so self-loving were iniquity*

**To love such a self would indeed
be a sin.**

9 *'Tis thee, my self, that for myself I praise*

**It is you, my (other) self, that makes
me praise myself.**

10 *Painting my age with beauty of thy days*

**Describing my condition as though
it had your youthful beauty**

62

Sin of self-love possesseth° all mine eye, *occupies*
And all my soul, and all my every part;
And for this sin there is no remedy,
It is so grounded inward[1] in my heart.   4
Methinks no face so gracious is as mine,[2]
No shape so true, no truth of such account,[3]
And for myself mine own worth do define
As I all other in all worths surmount.[4]   8
But when my glass° shows me myself indeed,[5] *mirror*
Beated° and chopped° with tanned antiquity,[6] *Beaten / cracked*
Mine own self-love quite contrary I read;[7]
Self so self-loving were iniquity.[8]   12
  'Tis thee, my self, that for myself I praise,[9]
  Painting my age with beauty of thy days.[10]

1   *Against*

   In anticipation of the day when

2   *traveled*

   (1) Journeyed; (2) toiled; travailed

3   *Stealing away*

   (1) Robbing him of; (2) fleeing with

4   *For*

   In preparation for

5   *fortify*

   Construct a defense

6   *though my lover's life*

   Although he will take *my lover's life*

7   *black lines*

   Lines of poetry

8   *in them still green*

   In these verses he will remain
   always young.

63

Against[1] my love shall be as I am now,

worn out With time's injurious hand crushed and o'erworn;°

When hours have drained his blood and filled his
brow

With lines and wrinkles; when his youthful morn 4

steep; precipitous Hath traveled[2] on to age's steepy° night,

And all those beauties whereof now he's king

Are vanishing or vanished out of sight,

i.e., youth Stealing away[3] the treasure of his spring;° 8

For[4] such a time do I now fortify[5]

destructive Against confounding° age's cruel knife,

So that That° he shall never cut from memory

My sweet love's beauty, though my lover's life.[6] 12

His beauty shall in these black lines[7] be seen,

And they shall live, and he in them still green.[8]

1   *The rich proud cost of outworn buried age*

    The lavish expenditures of antiquity

2   *And brass eternal slave to mortal rage*

    **And durable brass become vulner-
    able to human destruction**

3   *the hungry ocean gain / Advantage on the
    kingdom of the shore*

    **The surging ocean wear away the
    shore**

4   *win of the wat'ry main*

    Take from the ocean

5   *Increasing store with loss, and loss with
    store*

    **Adding to the stock of one the
    losses of the other**

6   *interchange of state*

    **(1) Shifting conditions; (2) political
    vicissitudes**

7   *state itself confounded to decay*

    Existence itself utterly destroyed

8   *cannot choose / But weep to have that
    which it fears to lose*

    **Cannot do anything but *weep*
    because it has what it is terrified to
    lose (i.e., love)**

64

cruel   When I have seen by time's fell° hand defaced
              The rich proud cost of outworn buried age;[1]
once / demolished   When sometime° lofty towers I see down-razed,°
              And brass eternal slave to mortal rage;[2]   4
              When I have seen the hungry ocean gain
              Advantage on the kingdom of the shore,[3]
              And the firm soil win of the wat'ry main,[4]
              Increasing store with loss, and loss with store;[5]   8
              When I have seen such interchange of state,[6]
              Or state itself confounded to decay,[7]
by this   Ruin hath taught me thus° to ruminate:
              That time will come and take my love away.   12
               This thought is as a death, which cannot choose
               But weep to have that which it fears to lose.[8]

1   *But sad mortality o'ersways their power*

I.e., whose strength is not overcome by the destructive action of
time

2   *How with this rage shall beauty hold a
plea*

How, against this destructive force,
can beauty prevail?

3   *action*

Influence (but also with the sense
of legal action)

4   *wrackful siege of batt'ring days*

Destructive assault of Time. (The
passage of time is likened to a bat-
tering ram, assaulting a castle or
fortification.)

5   *but Time decays*

That Time will ruin them (i.e., the
gates)

6   *Shall Time's best jewel from Time's chest
lie hid*

Will Time's favorite possession (i.e.,
the friend) be hidden safely from
Time's casket (i.e., a coffin)

7   *strong hand*

Powerful person (but with *black
ink* in line 14, *hand* belatedly might
suggest "handwriting")

8   *his swift foot*

Its (i.e., Time's) rapid advance

9   *who his spoil oe'r beauty can forbid*

Who can deny Time his victory over
beauty?

10   *have might*

Proves effective

11   *my love may still*

(1) My feelings of love, or (2) my
beloved may continue to

65

Since° brass, nor stone, nor earth, nor boundless sea,
But sad mortality o'ersways their power,[1]
How with this rage shall beauty hold a plea,[2]
Whose action[3] is no stronger than a flower?°   4
Oh, how shall summer's honey breath hold out
Against the wrackful siege of batt'ring days,[4]
When rocks impregnable° are not so stout,°
Nor gates of steel so strong, but Time decays?[5]   8
Oh, fearful meditation! Where, alack,°
Shall Time's best jewel from Time's chest lie hid?[6]
Or what strong hand[7] can hold his swift foot[8] back?
Or who his spoil oe'r beauty can forbid?[9]   12
  Oh, none, unless this miracle have might,[10]
  That in black ink my love may still[11] shine bright.

Since there is neither — (line 1)
i.e., flower's — (line 4)
invincible / sturdy — (line 7)
alas — (line 9)

1   *As to behold desert a beggar born*

For example, seeing worthy people born into poverty

2   *needy nothing trimmed in jollity*

Worthless people dressed in fine array

3   *purest faith unhappily forsworn*

Absolute devotion maliciously betrayed

4   *gilded honor shamefully misplaced*

Worthy titles granted undeservingly

5   *maiden virtue rudely strumpeted*

Chaste virtue falsely accused of being immoral

6   *limping sway disablèd*

Crippled by weak leaders

7   *art made tongue-tied by authority*

Learning or literature silenced by those in power, i.e., censored

8   *folly, doctor-like, controlling skill*

Idiocy, pretending to be a learned doctor, in authority over real expertise

9   *simple truth miscalled simplicity*

Plain truth disparaged as ignorance

10   *captive good attending captain ill*

Goodness forced to wait upon evil

11   *Save that to die, I leave my love alone*

Except that if I die I leave my beloved on his own (or, possibly, "the only thing I leave is my beloved")

66

Tired with all these,° for restful death I cry,
As to behold desert a beggar born,[1]
And needy nothing trimmed in jollity,[2]
And purest faith unhappily forsworn,[3]   4
And gilded honor shamefully misplaced,[4]
And maiden virtue rudely strumpeted,[5]
And right° perfection wrongfully disgraced, *genuine*
And strength by limping sway disablèd,[6]   8
And art made tongue-tied by authority,[7]
And folly, doctor-like, controlling skill,[8]
And simple truth miscalled simplicity,[9]
And captive good attending captain ill.[10]   12
  Tired with all these, from these would I be gone,
  Save that to die, I leave my love alone.[11]

1   *wherefore with infection*

    **Why around such (moral) corrup-
    tion**

2   *grace impiety*

    Make sin seem attractive

3   *lace itself with his society*

    **(1) Adorn itself with his presence;
    (2) work its way into his company**

4   *false painting imitate*

    **The use of cosmetics allow others
    to mimic**

5   *steal dead seeing*

    Appropriate the lifeless semblance

6   *poor beauty indirectly seek / Roses of
    shadow*

    **Inferior beauty look to imitation
    roses (i.e., cosmetics)**

7   *now Nature bankrupt is*

    **Now that Nature has no more
    beauty to bestow (having used it all
    upon the friend)**

8   *Beggared of blood to blush through lively
    veins*

    **Lacking blood for adding fresh
    color to vital young faces**

9   *And, proud of many, lives upon his gains*

    **Though boasting of her many
    beauties, nourishes herself on his
    excellence**

10 *In days long since, before these last so bad*

    **In times long past, before these
    troubled recent ones**

67

Ah, wherefore with infection[1] should he live
And with his presence grace impiety,[2]
So that That° sin by him advantage should achieve
And lace itself with his society?[3]   4
Why should false painting imitate[4] his cheek
And steal dead seeing[5] of his living hue?
Why should poor beauty indirectly seek
natural Roses of shadow,[6] since his rose is true?°   8
Why should he live, now Nature bankrupt is,[7]
Beggared of blood to blush through lively veins,[8]
treasury For she hath no exchequer° now but his,
And, proud of many, lives upon his gains?[9]   12
preserves Oh, him she stores,° to show what wealth she had
In days long since, before these last so bad.[10]

1   *as flowers do now*

I.e., without cosmetics; naturally

2   *bastard signs of fair*

False displays of beauty, i.e.,
cosmetics

3   *born*

(1) Invented; (2) borne, i.e., worn or
displayed

4   *durst inhabit on*

Dared to dwell upon

5   *tresses of the dead*

Hair of dead people (which was
used to make wigs)

6   *right of sepulchers*

Rightfully the possessions of tombs

7   *beauty's dead fleece*

The hair of a dead beauty

8   *holy antique hours*

Venerable days gone by

9   *itself and true*

I.e., natural and unadorned

10 *Making no summer of another's green*

Not making beauty out of someone
else's youth

11 *Robbing no old*

Stealing no old thing

12 *as for a map doth nature store*

To function as a model (see *map*
in line 1) nature (1) fills him with
beauty, or (2) preserves him.

13 *false art*

Deception, i.e., cosmetics or wigs

14 *of yore*

In days past (with *yore* possibly sug-
gesting "your")

68

Thus is his cheek the map° of days outworn,   *picture; embodiment*
When beauty lived and died as flowers do now,[1]
Before these bastard signs of fair[2] were born,[3]
Or durst inhabit on[4] a living brow;   4
Before the golden tresses of the dead,[5]
The right of sepulchers,[6] were shorn away,
To live a second life on second head,
Ere beauty's dead fleece[7] made another gay.°   *attractive*   8
In him those holy antique hours[8] are seen,
Without all° ornament, itself and true,[9]   *any*
Making no summer of another's green,[10]
Robbing no old[11] to dress his beauty new;   12
 And him as for a map doth nature store,[12]
 To show false art[13] what beauty was of yore.[14]

1   *parts*

(1) Physical attributes; (2) personal
qualities

2   *thought of hearts can mend*

Heartfelt imagination could improve upon

3   *Utt'ring bare truth, even so as foes*
commend

Speaking the plain truth, so that
even your enemies praise you

4   *Thy outward thus with outward praise is*
crowned

Your visible appearance is thus
rewarded with public admiration.

5   *so thine own*

What is yours; what you deserve

6   *In other accents do this praise confound*

In less kind tones contradict this
praise

7   *the eye hath shown*

I.e., what *the world's eye* (line 1) can
see

8   *look into*

Scrutinize

9   *And that, in guess, they measure by thy*
deeds

And that (i.e., the beauty of your
mind), they estimate by measuring
your actions

10 *churls their thoughts*

I.e., their churlish thoughts

11 *To thy fair flower add the rank smell of*
weeds

To your lovely appearance add
the corrupt smell of weeds. (As in
Sonnet 54, scent is likened to inner
virtue, in contrast to the flower's
outward appearance.)

12 *The soil is this, that thou dost common*
grow.

The root of the matter is this: you
have become vulgar.

69

Those parts[1] of thee that the world's eye doth view

Lack Want° nothing that the thought of hearts can mend.[2]

All tongues, the voice of souls, give thee that due,

Utt'ring bare truth, even so as foes commend.[3]   4

Thy outward thus with outward praise is crowned,[4]

But those same tongues that give thee so thine own[5]

In other accents do this praise confound[6]

By seeing farther than the eye hath shown.[7]   8

They look into[8] the beauty of thy mind,

And that, in guess, they measure by thy deeds;[9]

Then, churls their thoughts[10] (although their eyes
    were kind)

To thy fair flower add the rank smell of weeds.[11]   12

appearance   But why thy odor matcheth not thy show,°

    The soil is this, that thou dost common grow.[12]

1   *That thou art blamed shall not be thy defect*

   It is not your fault that you are criticized.

2   *was ever yet the fair*

   Has always been the beautiful

3   *The ornament of beauty is suspect*

   Suspicion inevitably accompanies beauty.

4   *A crow*

   Bird considered by the ancients to be a bad omen; hence, a black mark on the beautiful heavens

5   *slander doth but approve / Thy worth the greater*

   Slander only proves you more worthy.

6   *being wooed of time*

   Since you have been favored by time (in being beautiful)

7   *canker vice*

   Vice, which is like a cankerworm (caterpillar, which proverbally eats the prettiest flowers)

8   *present'st a pure unstainèd prime*

   Exhibit the unblemished innocence of early adulthood

9   *the ambush of young days*

   The traps waiting to ensnare youth

10 *Either not assailed, or victor being charged*

   Either not tempted, or being able to resist the tempation

11 *Yet this thy praise cannot be so thy praise / To tie up envy evermore enlarged*

   Yet this praise of you cannot be so great as to restrain the envy that is continually provoked (by your beauty).

12 *If some suspect of ill masked not thy show, / Then thou alone kingdoms of hearts shouldst owe.*

   If some hint of wickedness did not cloud your appearance, you alone would own (owe) the hearts of many kingdoms.

70

That thou art blamed shall not be thy defect,[1]

target For slander's mark° was ever yet the fair;[2]

The ornament of beauty is suspect,[3]

A crow[4] that flies in Heaven's sweetest air.   4

Provided that So° thou be good, slander doth but approve

Thy worth the greater,[5] being wooed of time;[6]

For canker vice[7] the sweetest buds doth love,

And thou present'st a pure unstainèd prime.[8]   8

Thou hast passed by the ambush of young days,[9]

Either not assailed, or victor being charged;[10]

Yet this thy praise cannot be so thy praise

To tie up envy evermore enlarged.[11]   12

 If some suspect of ill masked not thy show,

 Then thou alone kingdoms of hearts shouldst owe.[12]

1   *No longer mourn for me when I am dead /*
    Than you shall hear the surly sullen bell

    **After I have died, do not mourn for
    me any longer than you can hear
    the somber sound of my funeral
    bells.**

2   *so*

    (1) In such a manner; (2) so much

3   *I in your sweet thoughts would be forgot*

    **Would like your *sweet thoughts* to
    forget me**

4   *make you woe*

    Cause you to feel sad

5   *compounded am with clay*

    **Have become one with the earth
    (i.e., am dead and buried)**

6   *even with my life decay*

    Die at the same time as my life

7   *look into your moan*

    Investigate your grief

8   *mock you with me*

    **(1) Scorn you for loving me; (2) scorn
    you along with me**

71

No longer mourn for me when I am dead
Than you shall hear the surly sullen bell [1]
notice Give warning° to the world that I am fled
From this vile world with vilest worms to dwell.   4
Nay, if you read this line, remember not
The hand that writ it, for I love you so [2]
That I in your sweet thoughts would be forgot, [3]
about If thinking on° me then should make you woe. [4]   8
Oh, if, I say, you look upon this verse
When I perhaps compounded am with clay, [5]
repeat; speak Do not so much as my poor name rehearse, °
But let your love even with my life decay, [6]   12
 Lest the wise world should look into your moan [7]
 And mock you with me [8] after I am gone.

1   *task you to recite*

    Assign you the chore of telling

2   *What merit lived in me that you should love / After my death*

    What virtues I possessed so that you continue to love me after I have died

3   *you in me can nothing worthy prove*

    You cannot show that there was anything of value in my life.

4   *mine own desert*

    What I actually deserve

5   *hang more praise*

    Alludes to the practice of hanging trophies or honors on the tombs of soldiers or great men

6   *lest your true love may seem false in this*

    To prevent your true love from seeming to lie about this (i.e., my qualities)

7   *That you for love speak well of me untrue*

    That out of love you compliment me undeservingly

8   *My name*

    Let my name (i.e., my reputation)

9   *bring forth*

    Have accomplished (i.e., these poems)

10 *so should you, to love things nothing worth*

    You should be ashamed, too, to love things of no value.

72

Oh, lest the world should task you to recite [1]
What merit lived in me that you should love
After my death, [2] dear love, forget me quite,
For you in me can nothing worthy prove; [3]   4
Unless you would devise some virtuous lie,
To do more for me than mine own desert, [4]
And hang more praise [5] upon deceasèd I
stingy / relate Than niggard° truth would willingly impart.°   8
Oh, lest your true love may seem false in this, [6]
That you for love speak well of me untrue, [7]
My name [8] be buried where my body is,
neither And live no more to shame nor° me nor you.   12
  For I am shamed by that which I bring forth, [9]
  And so should you, to love things nothing worth. [10]

1   *shake against*

    Shiver in expectation of (or "in the
    face of ")

2   *choirs*

    The choir is the area of a church to
    the east of the nave set aside for the
    choristers. (*Choirs,* spelled "quiers"
    in Q, can also mean sheaves of
    paper, particularly the gatherings
    of sheets to be bound for a book,
    and so, with *leaves* in line 2, hints at
    the sense of writings now old and
    ineffective.)

3   *Death's second self, that seals up all*

    I.e., sleep, that encloses the day, or
    sews eyes shut (to "seel" is to sew
    shut the eyes of a hawk or falcon),
    or seals up everything, as one
    would fold and seal a letter.

4   *Consumed with that which it was*
    nourished by

    I.e., put out by the ashes of the
    once-glowing fire of his youth

5   *that*

    (1) Me, the poet; (2) life itself

6   *leave*

    (1) Give up; (2) depart from

73

That time of year thou mayst in me behold
When yellow leaves, or none, or few, do hang
Upon those boughs which shake against[1] the cold,
formerly   Bare ruined choirs,[2] where late° the sweet birds sang.   4
In me thou see'st the twilight of such day
As after sunset fadeth in the west,
Which by and by black night doth take away,
Death's second self, that seals up all[3] in rest.   8
In me thou see'st the glowing of such fire
That on the ashes of his youth doth lie,
As the deathbed whereon it must expire
Consumed with that which it was nourished by.[4]   12
  This thou perceiv'st, which makes thy love more strong,
  To love that[5] well which thou must leave[6] ere long.

1   *that fell arrest / Without all bail*

I.e., when cruel (*fell*) irresistible death

2   *My life hath in this line some interest*

My life has some investment in this line of verse.

3   *for memorial*

(1) To aid your memory; (2) as a monument

4   *The very part was consecrate to thee*

The exact part of me that was devoted to you (i.e., *my spirit* in line 8)

5   *earth can have but earth*

An echo of the Elizabethan burial service: "earth to earth, ashes to ashes, dust to dust"

6   *the dregs*

Literally, the residue that sinks to the bottom of wine

7   *The coward conquest of a wretch's knife*

Coward might refer to either the dying man or the *wretch* (perhaps a personification of Death).

8   *Too base of thee to be rememberèd*

Too worthless to be remembered by you

9   *The worth of that is that which it contains*

The body's worth lies in what is inside it (i.e., the spirit)

74

But be contented° when that fell arrest   *untroubled; resigned*
Without all bail[1] shall carry me away;
My life hath in this line some interest,[2]
Which for memorial[3] still with thee shall stay.   4
When thou reviewest° this, thou dost review   *reexamine*
The very part was consecrate to thee.[4]
The earth can have but earth,[5] which is his° due;   *its*
My spirit is thine, the better part of me.   8
So then thou hast but° lost the dregs[6] of life,   *only*
The prey of worms, my body being dead,
The coward conquest of a wretch's knife,[7]
Too base of thee to be rememberèd.[8]   12
  The worth of that is that which it contains,[9]
  And that is this,° and this with thee remains.   *this poem*

1   *So are you to my thoughts as food to life*

You nourish my thoughts as food does life.

2   *sweet seasoned*

(1) In the pleasant time of year, i.e., spring; (2) *sweet* smelling

3   *And for the peace of you I hold such strife*

In order to enjoy the contentment I feel in your company, I suffer the anxiety

4   *Now proud as an enjoyer, and anon / Doubting the filching age will steal his treasure*

At one moment taking pleasure in the possession of his wealth, and the next, afraid that this criminal age will rob him of it.

5   *counting best*

Thinking it best

6   *Then bettered*

Then thinking it would be even better

7   *Save what is had or must from you be took*

Except what is received or must be taken from you

8   *pine and surfeit*

Starve or binge

9   *Or gluttoning on all, or all away*

Either feasting on everything or having nothing at all

75

So are you to my thoughts as food to life,[1]
Or as sweet seasoned[2] showers are to the ground;
And for the peace of you I hold such strife[3]
As 'twixt a miser and his wealth is found;   4
Now proud as an enjoyer, and anon
Doubting the filching age will steal his treasure;[4]
Now counting best[5] to be with you alone,
Then bettered[6] that the world may see my pleasure.   8
At times Sometime° all full with feasting on your sight
completely And by and by clean° starvèd for a look,
Possessing or pursuing no delight
Save what is had or must from you be took.[7]   12
  Thus do I pine and surfeit[8] day by day,
  Or gluttoning on all, or all away.[9]

1 *barren of new pride*

   **Deficient in fashionable ornamen-
   tation**

2 *quick change*

   Lively diversity

3 *Why with the time do I not glance aside /
   To new-found methods and to compounds
   strange?*

   **Why don't I, as everyone else does
   nowadays, turn to new ways (of
   writing) and newly minted words?**

4 *Why write I still all one*

   Why do I always write only one way

5 *invention in a noted weed*

   **Imagination in familiar dress (i.e.,
   in the same literary style)**

6 *tell my name*

   Reveals that I am its author

7 *all my best is dressing old words new*

   **The best I can do is spruce up *old
   words*.**

8 *daily new and old*

   Rises and sets every day

9 *still telling what is told*

   **Continually saying what has already
   been said**

76

Why is my verse so barren of new pride,[1]
So far from variation or quick change?[2]
Why with the time do I not glance aside
To new-found methods and to compounds strange?[3]   4
Why write I still all one,[4] ever the same,
And keep invention in a noted weed,[5]
That every word doth almost tell my name,[6]
Showing their birth,° and where° they did proceed?   8

heritage / from where

Oh, know, sweet love, I always write of you,
And you and love are still my argument.°

subject matter

So all my best is dressing old words new,[7]
Spending again what is already spent: 12
  For as the sun is daily new and old,[8]
  So is my love still telling what is told.[9]

1   *waste*

(1) Dwindle; (2) are squandered

2   *vacant leaves*

Blank pages (perhaps of a notebook in which the friend can write)

3   *this learning mayst thou taste*

You may experience the following lesson.

4   *Of mouthèd graves will give thee memory*

Will remind you of devouring graves

5   *Thou by thy dial's shady stealth mayst know*

By the shadow's slow movement (across the sundial) you may recognize

6   *Time's thievish progress*

Time's theft of each moment

7   *Look what*

Whatever

8   *Commit to these waste blanks*

Write down on these blank pages

9   *Those children nursed*

Your thoughts taken care of (as children often were by a nurse)

10 *To take a new acquaintance of thy mind*

I.e., and ready now to be reintroduced to you

11 *These offices*

These actions (i.e., all the actions suggested in lines 1–12)

77

Thy glass° will show thee how thy beauties wear,° — *mirror / wear out; age*
Thy dial° how thy precious minutes waste,[1] — *sundial*
The vacant leaves[2] thy mind's imprínt will bear,
And of° this book this learning mayst thou taste:[3] — *from*   4
The wrinkles which thy glass will truly show
Of mouthèd graves will give thee memory;[4]
Thou by thy dial's shady stealth mayst know[5]
Time's thievish progress[6] to eternity.   8
Look what[7] thy memory cannot contain,
Commit to these waste blanks,[8] and thou shalt find
Those children nursed,[9] delivered° from thy brain, — *once delivered*
To take a new acquaintance of thy mind.[10]   12
  These offices,[11] so oft as thou wilt look,
  Shall profit thee and much enrich thy book.

1   *fair assistance*

Inspiration from your fair appearance

2   *As every alien pen hath got my use / And under thee their poesy disperse*

That all other poets have taken my cue and similarly inspired by you put forth their verse

3   *the dumb on high to sing*

The mute to sing (1) loudly; (2) to the heavens

4   *Have added feathers to the learnèd's wing*

I.e., have provided additional inspiration for the other poets

5   *And given grace a double majesty*

And doubled the excellence of their talents

6   *Whose influence is thine and born of thee*

The qualities of which derive from and are determined by you (as stars exert astrological control over the lives of men).

7   *And arts with thy sweet graces gracèd be*

And your loveliness inspires their poetic ornament

8   *But thou art all my art, and dost advance / As high as learning my rude ignorance.*

But you provide the essence of my writing (not just its style), and raise my ordinary talent to the height of poetic skill.

78

to be So oft have I invoked thee for° my muse
And found such fair assistance[1] in my verse,
As every alien pen hath got my use
And under thee their poesy disperse.[2]   4
Thine eyes, that taught the dumb on high to sing,[3]
And heavy ignorance aloft to fly,
Have added feathers to the learnèd's wing[4]
And given grace a double majesty.[5]   8
compose Yet be most proud of that which I compile,°
Whose influence is thine and born of thee.[6]
improve In others' works thou dost but mend° the style,
And arts with thy sweet graces gracèd be.[7]   12
  But thou art all my art, and dost advance
  As high as learning my rude ignorance.[8]

1   *My verse alone had all thy gentle grace*

    **Only my poetry (1) enjoyed your
    patronage; (2) contained all of your
    lovely graces.**

2   *gracious numbers*

    **(1) Graceful verses; (2) verses
    describing your *gracious* qualities**

3   *my sick muse doth give another place*

    **My decaying poetic gifts make
    room for another (poet).**

4   *lovely argument / Deserves the travail of
    a worthier pen*

    **The sweet topic (of your beauty)
    deserves the efforts of a better
    writer.**

5   *Yet what of thee thy poet doth invent / He
    robs thee of and pays it thee again*

    **But that which your (new) poet
    writes about you is merely stolen
    from you and then repaid to you
    again.**

6   *afford*

    **(1) Offer you; (2) have the means to
    pay for**

7   *thou thyself dost pay*

    You have yourself provided

79

At the time when Whilst° I alone did call upon thy aid,
My verse alone had all thy gentle grace,[1]
But now my gracious numbers[2] are decayed,
And my sick muse doth give another place.[3]   4
I grant, sweet love, thy lovely argument
Deserves the travail of a worthier pen;[4]
Yet what of thee thy poet doth invent
He robs thee of and pays it thee again.[5]   8
ascribes to He lends° thee virtue, and he stole that word
From thy behavior; beauty doth he give
And found it in thy cheek. He can afford[6]
No praise to thee but what in thee doth live;   12
  Then thank him not for that which he doth say,
  Since what he owes thee thou thyself dost pay.[7]

1   *a better spirit*

(1) A more inspired poet; (2) a
superior soul

2   *use your name*

(1) Take you for his inspiration; (2)
exploit you

3   *The humble as the proudest sail doth bear*

Carries the smallest as well as the
grandest ship

4   *saucy bark*

Audacious little boat

5   *broad main*

Spacious expanse (of water)

6   *shallowest help*

Smallest support (i.e., since the
speaker imagines his poetry to be
only a small ship, the shallowest
waters will accommodate him)

7   *Or, being wracked*

(1) Or if I am wrecked; (2) since I am
already ruined

8   *He of tall building and of goodly pride*

While he (is) grand in stature (high-
masted) and of splendid bearing

9   *The worst was this: my love was my decay*

The greatest pain was this: the
cause of my ruin was (1) my beloved;
(2) my affection.

80

Oh, how I faint° when I of you do write,   *lose heart; falter*
Knowing a better spirit[1] doth use your name,[2]
And in the praise thereof° spends all his might   *(of your name)*
To make me tongue-tied speaking of your fame.   4
But since your worth, wide as the ocean is,
The humble as the proudest sail doth bear,[3]
My saucy bark,[4] inferior far to his,
On your broad main[5] doth willfully° appear.   *boldly*   8
Your shallowest help[6] will hold me up afloat,
Whilst he upon your soundless° deep doth ride,   *unfathomable*
Or, being wracked,[7] I am a worthless boat,
He of tall building and of goodly pride.[8]   12
  Then, if he thrive and I be cast away,
  The worst was this: my love was my decay.[9]

1   *Or I shall live your epitaph to make*

**Whether I live to write your epitaph
(i.e., outlive you)**

2   *From hence your memory death cannot
take*

**From here (this world; this verse)
death cannot erase remembrance
of you.**

3   *in me each part*

Each part of me

4   *from hence*

**(1) From this point on; (2) from these
sonnets**

5   *to all the world*

To all posterity

6   *a common grave*

**(1) A simple grave; (2) a grave shared
with others**

7   *entombèd in men's eyes*

**Buried in readers' eyes (with a pun
on "tome," a large book**

8   *Your monument shall be my gentle verse*

**My *gentle verse* will serve as your me-
morial. (*Gentle* here means "tender"
but also carries its social sense,
"honorable" or "noble," a quality
taken over from the friend and
contrasting with the *common grave*
the poet imagines for himself.)**

9   *And tongues to-be your being shall
rehearse*

**And the tongues of those who have
not yet been born will recall your
existence**

10   *You still shall live*

**(1) You will continue to live; (2) you
will live nonetheless**

11   *Where breath most breathes, even in the
mouths of men*

**Wherever *breath* is most vital, that
is, in the speech of living men**

81

Or I shall live your epitaph to make,[1]
Or you survive when I in earth am rotten,
From hence your memory death cannot take,[2]
Although in me each part[3] will be forgotten.   4
Your name from hence[4] immortal life shall have,
Though I, once gone, to all the world[5] must die.
provide/only   The earth can yield° me but° a common grave,[6]
When you entombèd in men's eyes[7] shall lie.   8
Your monument shall be my gentle verse,[8]
Which eyes not yet created shall o'er-read,
And tongues to-be your being shall rehearse[9]
living   When all the breathers° of this world are dead.   12
power   You still shall live[10]—such virtue° hath my pen—
Where breath most breathes, even in the mouths of
men.[11]

1   *I grant thou wert not married to my muse*

    I admit you are not obliged to read
    only my poetry.

2   *dedicated words*

    (1) Lines dedicating a work to
    another; (2) words of devotion

3   *blessing every book*

    The dedicated words bless either the
    books or *their fair subject*.

4   *fair in knowledge as in hue*

    Wise as you are handsome

5   *a limit past my praise*

    Beyond my ability to praise

6   *art enforced*

    You are forced

7   *fresher stamp of the time-bettering days*

    More up-to-date creation of these
    days in which literature is so
    improved

8   *And do so, love*

    (1) Do seek new poets, my love; (2)
    go ahead and love in this way

9   *strainèd touches*

    Forced or unnatural flourishes

10 *truly sympathized*

    Accurately depicted

11 *In true plain words by thy true-telling
    friend*

    In simple, unadorned words writ-
    ten by your sincere friend.

12 *gross painting*

    (1) Overly elaborate description; (2)
    exaggerated flattery. (Both senses
    are imagined as thickly applied
    cosmetics.)

13 *Where cheeks need blood*

    For one whose face lacks beauty

14 *in thee it is abused*

    Such rhetoric describing you is
    unnecessary.

82

I grant thou wert not married to my muse,[1]
And therefore mayst without attaint° o'erlook°
The dedicated words[2] which writers use
Of° their fair subject, blessing every book.[3]   4
Thou art as fair in knowledge as in hue,[4]
Finding thy worth a limit past my praise,[5]
And therefore art enforced[6] to seek anew
Some fresher stamp of the time-bettering days.[7]   8
And do so, love;[8] yet when they have devised
What strainèd touches[9] rhetoric can lend,
Thou, truly fair, wert truly sympathized[10]
In true plain words by thy true-telling friend.[11]   12
  And their gross painting[12] might be better used
  Where cheeks need blood;[13] in thee it is abused.[14]

ishonor / read; look over

About

1 *painting*

   (1) Cosmetics; (2) exaggerated praise

2 *to your fair no painting set*

   I added no adornment to your beauty.

3 *The barren tender of a poet's debt*

   The worthless benefit of what a poet is obliged to furnish (i.e., praise)

4 *have I slept in your report*

   I have been remiss in describing you.

5 *might show / How far a modern quill doth come too short, / Speaking of worth, what worth in you doth grow*

   Might demonstrate the inadequacy of any living poet to express the value that flourishes in you

6 *This silence for my sin you did impute*

   You considered this silence to be my sin.

7 *For I impair not beauty, being mute*

   Because I do not diminish your beauty, staying silent

8 *When others would give life, and bring a tomb*

   While other poets attempt to make your beauty live in their poetry, but actually deaden it

9 *both your poets*

   Most likely Shakespeare and a rival poet (see Sonnets 78, 80, and 86)

83

I never saw° that you did painting[1] need,   *i.e., thought*
And therefore to your fair no painting set.[2]
I found, or thought I found, you did exceed
The barren tender of a poet's debt.[3]   4
And therefore have I slept in your report,[4]
That° you yourself, being extant,° well might show   *So that / alive now*
How far a modern quill doth come too short,
Speaking of worth, what worth in you doth grow.[5]   8
This silence for my sin you did impute,[6]
Which shall be most my glory, being dumb,°   *mute; silent*
For I impair not beauty, being mute,[7]
When others would give life, and bring a tomb.[8]   12
    There lives more life in one of your fair eyes
    Than both your poets[9] can in praise devise.

195

1   *Who is it that says most*
    Where is the extravagant flattering poet

2   *that you alone are you*
    That you alone have the unique virtue of being you

3   *In whose confine immurèd is the store /*
    Which should example where your equal grew
    Within whom is the abundance of qualities, which alone can provide a measure of your own worth

4   *Lean penury*
    Miserly poverty (of imagination)

5   *so dignifies his story*
    In doing so, adds worth to his writing

6   *And such a counterpart shall fame his wit*
    And this representation of you will make his poetry famous

7   *You to your beauteous blessings add a curse*
    You undermine your lovely gifts

8   *Being fond on praise, which makes your praises worse*
    Your craving for praise lessens the praise you both give and receive.

84

who   Who is it that says most,[1] which° can say more
Than this rich praise: that you alone are you,[2]
In whose confine immurèd is the store
Which should example where your equal grew?[3]   4
Lean penury[4] within that pen doth dwell
That to his subject lends not some small glory,
But he that writes of you, if he can tell
That you are you, so dignifies his story.[5]   8
Let him but copy what in you is writ,
Not making worse what nature made so clear,
And such a counterpart shall fame his wit,[6]
Making his style admirèd everywhere.   12
  You to your beauteous blessings add a curse,[7]
  Being fond on praise, which makes your praises
    worse.[8]

1   *in manners holds her still*

     Politely remains quiet

2   *comments of your praise, richly compiled*

     **Treatises praising you, elaborately
     written**

3   *Reserve their character with golden
     quill / And precious phrase by all the
     muses filed*

     **Are preserved in the ornate writing
     and lofty language polished by the
     muses**

4   *like unlettered clerk*

     I, like an illiterate church officer

5   *To every hymn that able spirit affords*

     **To each song of praise that a
     capable poet provides**

6   *In polished form of well-refinèd pen*

     **I.e., in a mature and sophisticated
     style**

7   *holds his rank before*

     **(My love) keeps its portion at the
     front of the line**

8   *Then others for the breath of words
     respect, / Me for my dumb thoughts,
     speaking in effect.*

     **Then esteem the others for their
     airy words, [but] value me for my
     unspoken thoughts that speak
     through my actions.**

85

My tongue-tied muse in manners holds her still,[1]
While comments of your praise, richly compiled,[2]
Reserve their character with golden quill
And precious phrase by all the muses filed.[3]   4
others I think good thoughts whilst other° write good words,
And like unlettered clerk[4] still cry "Amen"
To every hymn that able spirit affords[5]
In polished form of well-refinèd pen.[6]   8
Hearing you praised, I say "'Tis so; 'tis true,"
utmost And to the most° of praise add something more;
i.e., only in But that is in° my thought, whose love to you,
in last place Though words come hindmost,° holds his rank
    before.[7]   12
Then others for the breath of words respect,
Me for my dumb thoughts, speaking in effect.[8]

1   *the proud full sail*

    The inspiring grandeur (returning
    to the nautical imagery of Sonnet
    80)

2   *Bound for the prize*

    In search of the treasure

3   *That did my ripe thoughts in my brain
    inhearse*

    That kept my full-grown thoughts
    buried in my brain (rather than
    expressed in verse)

4   *Making their tomb the womb*

    Making a grave of the womb

5   *his spirit, by spirits*

    His poetic soul, by ghosts of dead
    writers (or his own creative powers)

6   *Above a mortal pitch*

    In a style greater than a mere
    mortal should be capable of

7   *struck me dead*

    Silenced me (i.e., stopped me from
    writing)

8   *compeers by night*

    Nightly companions

9   *affable familiar ghost*

    Friendly, servile spirit (see notes 5
    and 8)

10 *gulls him with intelligence*

    Deludes him with false information

11 *from thence*

    I.e., of the spirits of the night

12 *Then lacked I matter, that enfeebled mine*

    Then I had nothing to write about,
    (and) my poetry was *enfeebled* by
    that lack of subject matter

86

Was it the proud full sail[1] of his° great verse, *i.e., a rival poet*

Bound for the prize[2] of all-too-precious you,

That did my ripe thoughts in my brain inhearse,[3]

Making their tomb the womb[4] wherein they grew?   4

Was it his spirit, by spirits[5] taught to write

Above a mortal pitch,[6] that struck me dead?[7]

No, neither he, nor his compeers by night[8]

Giving him aid, my verse astonishèd.°   8 *silenced; struck down*

He, nor that affable familiar ghost[9]

Which nightly gulls him with intelligence,[10]

As victors of my silence cannot° boast.   *i.e., can*

I was not sick of° any fear from thence;[11]   12 *because of*

But when your countenance° filled up his line,   *face; favor*

Then lacked I matter, that enfeebled mine.[12]

1   *thou art too dear for my possessing*

(1) You are loved too much for me to have; (2) you are too precious for someone like me.

2   *like enough thou know'st thy estimate*

No doubt you know your value.

3   *The charter of thy worth gives thee releasing*

The privilege your merits afford you releases you (from any hold I have on you).

4   *My bonds in thee are all determinate*

My claims on you have expired.

5   *but by thy granting*

Except with your permission

6   *The cause of this fair gift in me is wanting*

I lack the merit to justify this lovely gift (of you).

7   *my patent back again is swerving*

My claim on you reverts to you.

8   *else mistaking*

You confused with someone else; you misunderstood

9   *upon misprison growing*

Based upon an inaccurate appraisal

10   *Comes home again, on better judgment making*

Returns to you, once you had second thoughts

11   *no such matter*

Nothing of the kind

87

Farewell; thou art too dear for my possessing,[1]
And like enough thou know'st thy estimate.[2]
The charter of thy worth gives thee releasing;[3]
My bonds in thee are all determinate.[4]   4
For how do I hold thee but by thy granting,[5]
wealth And for that riches° where is my deserving?
The cause of this fair gift in me is wanting,[6]
And so my patent back again is swerving.[7]   8
Thyself thou gav'st, thy own worth then not knowing,
Or me, to whom thou gav'st it, else mistaking;[8]
So thy great gift, upon misprision growing,[9]
Comes home again, on better judgment making.[10]   12
possessed / deceive   Thus have I had° thee as a dream doth flatter:°
In sleep a king, but waking no such matter.[11]

1   *set me light*

     Think me of little value

2   *place my merit in the eye of scorn*

     Hold my worth up to ridicule

3   *prove thee virtuous, though thou art
     forsworn*

     Show your honesty, though you
     have perjured yourself (by denying
     the *merit* you previously affirmed)

4   *Upon thy part I can set down a story / Of
     faults concealed, wherein I am attainted*

     To bolster your case, I can testify
     to the hidden faults that (1) I am cor-
     rupted by, or (2) I am accused of.

5   *Doing thee vantage, double vantage me*

     Doing you a favor, will doubly
     benefit me (i.e., because you and I
     are one, a benefit to you is also one
     to me, and because it will allow me
     to think about you).

6   *for thy right*

     (1) To establish your virtue; (2) an
     account of your virtue

7   *bear all wrong*

     (1) Endure all injury; (2) take respon-
     sibility for everything; (3) report
     everything incorrectly

88

When thou shalt be disposed to set me light[1]
And place my merit in the eye of scorn,[2]
Upon thy side against myself I'll fight
And prove thee virtuous, though thou art forsworn.[3]　　　4
With mine own weakness being best acquainted,
Upon thy part I can set down a story
Of faults concealed, wherein I am attainted,[4]
So that That° thou in losing me shall win much glory.　　　8
And I by this will be a gainer too,
focusing / to For bending° all my loving thoughts on° thee;
The injuries that to myself I do,
Doing thee vantage, double vantage me.[5]　　　12
so much; in such a manner Such is my love, to thee I so° belong,
That for thy right[6] myself will bear all wrong.[7]

1   *I straight will halt*

      I will immediately begin to limp.

2   *thy reasons*

      (1) Your arguments; (2) your reasons
      (for forsaking me)

3   *To set a form upon*

      In order to make plausible

4   *As I'll myself disgrace, knowing thy will*

      As I will discredit myself, knowing
      (1) what you want; (2) me, your Will
      Shakespeare

5   *I will acquaintance strangle and look
      strange*

      I will pretend we do not know each
      other and look at you as a stranger
      would.

6   *Be absent from thy walks*

      (I will) stay away from the places
      you go.

7   *too much profane*

      Too unworthy of you

8   *For thee against myself I'll vow debate*

      On your behalf I will fight my own
      desires.

89

Say° that thou didst forsake me for some fault,   *Assert*
And I will comment° upon that offense.   *elaborate*
Speak of my lameness, and I straight will halt,[1]
Against thy reasons[2] making no defense.   4
Thou canst not, love, disgrace° me half so ill,   *discredit*
To set a form upon[3] desirèd change,
As I'll myself disgrace, knowing thy will;[4]
I will acquaintance strangle and look strange,[5]   8
Be absent from thy walks,[6] and in my tongue
Thy sweet belovèd name no more shall dwell,
Lest I, too much profane,[7] should do it° wrong   *i.e., your name*
And haply° of our old acquaintance tell.   *by chance*   12
    For thee against myself I'll vow debate,[8]
    For I must ne'er love him whom thou dost hate.

1   *Then hate me when thou wilt, if ever, now*

Therefore hate me if you want to,
but if you are someday going to do
it, do it now.

2   *is bent my deeds to cross*

Is intent on spoiling everything I do

3   *do not drop in for an after-loss*

I.e., do not kick me when I am
already down.

4   *Come in the rearward of a conquered woe*

Come in like the rearguard of an
army to attack one already defeated

5   *Give not a windy night a rainy morrow*

Do not add to the trouble of a
stormy night a *rainy* morning.

6   *To linger out a purposed overthrow*

By dragging out the harm you
intend to inflict

7   *leave me last*

I.e., be the last of my
misfortunes (see note 1)

8   *When other petty griefs have done their
spite*

After lesser troubles have taken
their toll

90

Then hate me when thou wilt, if ever, now,[1]
Now, while the world is bent my deeds to cross,[2]
malice/submit Join with the spite° of fortune, make me bow,°
And do not drop in for an after-loss.[3] 4
i.e., recovered from Ah, do not, when my heart hath 'scaped° this sorrow,
Come in the rearward of a conquered woe.[4]
Give not a windy night a rainy morrow,[5]
To linger out a purposed overthrow.[6] 8
If thou wilt leave me, do not leave me last,[7]
When other petty griefs have done their spite,[8]
initial attack/experience But in the onset° come; so shall I taste°
At first the very worst of fortune's might, 12
types/painful And other strains° of woe, which now seem woe,°
i.e., so painful Compared with loss of thee will not seem so.°

1 *glory in*

    (1) Revel in; (2) boast of

2 *though new-fangled ill*

    However fashionably absurd

3 *humor*

    Taste; temperament

4 *particulars are not my measure*

    Personal preferences do not satisfy
    me.

5 *prouder than garments' cost*

    More impressive than the richness
    of expensive clothes

6 *of all men's pride I boast*

    I boast of having what every man
    would love to have.

91

Some glory in [1] their birth, some in their skill,° *knowledge*
Some in their wealth, some in their body's force,
Some in their garments, though new-fangled ill,[2]
Some in their hawks and hounds, some in their
      horse;° *horses*   4
And every humor[3] hath his° adjunct° pleasure, *its / corresponding*
Wherein it finds a joy above the rest.
But these particulars are not my measure;[4]
All these I better° in one general best. *outshine*   8
Thy love is better than high birth to me,
Richer than wealth, prouder than garments' cost,[5]
Of more delight than hawks or horses be;
And, having thee, of all men's pride I boast;[6]   12
   Wretched° in this alone: that thou mayst take *Unfotunate*
   All this away, and me most wretched make.

1   *But do thy worst to steal thyself away*

     **Even if you try your hardest to (1)
     sneak away; (2) rob me of you**

2   *For term of life thou art assurèd mine*

     **For my entire life you are contracted
     to me.**

3   *depends upon*

     **(1) Counts on; (2) is nourished only
     by**

4   *the worst of wrongs*

     I.e., you leaving me

5   *least of them*

     **I.e., the slightest sign of
     disapproval**

6   *Thou canst not vex me with inconstant
     mind, / Since that my life on thy revolt
     doth lie.*

     **You cannot trouble me with your
     fickle heart, since my life will end
     with a single change of your affec-
     tion.**

7   *But what's so blessèd-fair that fears no
     blot?*

     **What is so wonderful that cannot
     be tainted?**

8   *mayst*

     (1) May one day; (2) may already

92

But do thy worst to steal thyself away,[1]
For term of life thou art assurèd mine,[2]
And life° no longer than thy love will stay,°   *i.e., my life / remain*
For it depends upon[3] that love of thine.   4
Then need I not to fear the worst of wrongs,[4]
When in the least of them[5] my life hath end.
I see a better state to me belongs
Than that which on thy humor° doth depend.   *mood*   8
Thou canst not vex me with inconstant mind,
Since that my life on thy revolt doth lie.[6]
Oh, what a happy title° do I find,   *claim to you*
Happy to have thy love, happy to die!   12
  But what's so blessèd-fair that fears no blot?[7]
Thou mayst[8] be false,° and yet I know it not.   *unfaithful*

1   *So shall I live, supposing thou art true*

    **In this way I will live, believing that
    you are faithful.**

2   *though altered new*

    **Even though your feelings have
    recently changed**

3   *Thy looks with me, thy heart in other
    place*

    **I.e., you appear loving, but your
    affection is elsewhere**

4   *In many's looks, the false heart's history*

    **In the expressions of many men, a
    record of the unfaithful heart**

5   *in thy creation*

    In creating you

6   *but sweetness tell*

    Except kindness display

7   *How like Eve's apple doth thy beauty
    grow, / If thy sweet virtue answer not thy
    show.*

    **How similar to the deceptive apple
    from the biblical Garden of Eden
    does your beauty become, if your
    conduct does not match your ap-
    pearance.**

93

So shall I live, supposing thou art true,[1]
so that / appearance Like a deceivèd husband, so° love's face°
May still seem love to me, though altered new:[2]
Thy looks with me, thy heart in other place.[3]   4
For there can live no hatred in thine eye;
Therefore in that I cannot know thy change.
In many's looks, the false heart's history[4]
unfamiliar Is writ in moods and frowns and wrinkles strange,°   8
But Heaven in thy creation[5] did decree
That in thy face sweet love should ever dwell.
Whate'er thy thoughts or thy heart's workings be,
i.e., from your face Thy looks should nothing thence° but sweetness tell.[6]   12
　How like Eve's apple doth thy beauty grow,
　If thy sweet virtue answer not thy show.[7]

1   *they most do show*

    They seem most likely to do

2   *husband nature's riches from expense*

    Prevent these gifts from being
    wasted

3   *but stewards of their excellence*

    Merely custodians of their beauty
    (i.e., of the beauty of the *lords and
    owners* of it)

4   *The summer's flow'r is to the summer
    sweet, / Though to itself it only live and
    die.*

    I.e., the blooming *flower* imparts
    its beauty to the *summer*, though it
    keeps to itself alone.

5   *with base infection meet*

    Becomes diseased

6   *The basest weed outbraves his dignity*

    The most lowly *weed* surpasses its
    value.

7   *For sweetest things turn sourest by their
    deeds*

    The most beautiful beings may be
    corrupted by their actions.

8   *Lilies that fester smell far worse than
    weeds*

    I.e., Something beautiful gone bad
    is far more offensive than some-
    thing that was ugly to begin with.

94

They that have pow'r to hurt and will do none,
That do not do the thing they most do show,[1]
affecting; arousing Who, moving° others, are themselves as stone,
Unmovèd, cold, and to temptation slow,   4
gifts They rightly do inherit Heaven's graces°
And husband nature's riches from expense.[2]
appearances They are the lords and owners of their faces,°
Others but stewards of their excellence.[3]   8
The summer's flow'r is to the summer sweet,
Though to itself it only live and die.[4]
But if that flow'r with base infection meet,[5]
The basest weed outbraves his dignity: [6]   12
  For sweetest things turn sourest by their deeds;[7]
  Lilies that fester smell far worse than weeds.[8]

1   *the beauty of thy budding name*

      **The perfection of your blossoming
      reputation**

2   *That tongue*

      Whatever person

3   *Naming thy name blesses an ill report*

      **Merely speaking your name turns
      criticism into praise.**

4   *all things turns to fair that eyes can see*

      **(*Beauty's veil*) makes everything
      seem lovely.**

5   *large privilege*

      Unrestricted freedom

95

How sweet and lovely° dost thou make the shame, *beautiful; lovable*

Which, like a canker° in the fragrant rose, *cankerworm*

Doth spot° the beauty of thy budding name! [1] *tarnish*

Oh, in what sweets° dost thou thy sins enclose! 4 *sweet fragrances*

That tongue [2] that tells the story of thy days,

Making lascivious comments on thy sport,° *entertainment*

Cannot dispraise, but,° in a kind of praise, *except*

Naming thy name blesses an ill report. [3] 8

Oh, what a mansion° have those vices got *dwelling*

Which for their habitation° chose out thee, *home*

Where beauty's veil doth cover every blot,° *fault*

And all things turns to fair that eyes can see! [4] 12

Take heed, dear heart, of this large privilege; [5]

The hardest knife ill used doth lose his° edge. *its*

1   *gentle sport*

     Good fun

2   *of more and less*

     By upper- and lower-class people

3   *Thou mak'st faults graces that to thee
     resort*

     **You turn flaws into charms when
     they are yours.**

4   *for true things deemed*

     Considered to be virtuous qualities

5   *If like a lamb he could his looks translate*

     **If he could transform his appear-
     ance into a lamb's**

6   *How many gazers mightst thou lead away*

     **How many admirers could you
     seduce**

7   *the strength of all thy state*

     All the charisma you possess

8   *As, thou being mine, mine is thy good
     report*

     **Since you are my beloved, my
     reputation depends on yours. (Son-
     net 36 concludes with this same
     couplet.)**

96

lasciviousness	Some say thy fault is youth, some wantonness,°
charm	Some say thy grace° is youth and gentle sport.[1]
	Both grace and faults are loved of more and less;[2]
	Thou mak'st faults graces that to thee resort.[3] 4
	As on the finger of a thronèd queen
most common	The basest° jewel will be well esteemed,
	So are those errors that in thee are seen
transformed	To truths translated,° and for true things deemed.[4] 8
fierce	How many lambs might the stern° wolf betray,
	If like a lamb he could his looks translate?[5]
	How many gazers mightst thou lead away[6]
	If thou wouldst use the strength of all thy state?[7] 12
do so / a way	But do not so.° I love thee in such sort,°
	As, thou being mine, mine is thy good report.[8]

1   *the pleasure of the fleeting year*

Who are my source of pleasure in
the swiftly passing year

2   *old December's bareness*

The barreness of late December

3   *this time removed was summer's time*

The time I was away was summer
(which here extends through the
harvest).

4   *The teeming autumn big with rich
increase*

The fertile autumn, brimming with
what is ready to be harvested

5   *Bearing the wanton burden of the prime*

Carrying (as if pregnant) the prog-
eny of the amorous spring

6   *Like widowed wombs after their lords'
decease*

Like pregnant widows do after their
husbands die. (The spring is compared to a lustful father, who has
died, leaving summer pregnant and
to give birth in autumn's harvest.)

7   *But hope of orphans and unfathered fruit*

Like the dashed hopes of orphans
and fatherless children

8   *wait on thee*

Serve you

9   *thou away, the very birds are mute*

When you are away even the birds
stop singing.

10 *with so dull a cheer*

I.e., so mournfully

97

How like a winter hath my absence been
From thee, the pleasure of the fleeting year![1]
What freezings have I felt, what dark days seen,
What old December's bareness[2] everywhere!   4
And yet this time removed was summer's time,[3]
The teeming autumn big with rich increase,[4]
Bearing the wanton burden of the prime,[5]
Like widowed wombs after their lords' decease.[6]   8
offspring   Yet this abundant issue° seemed to me
But hope of orphans and unfathered fruit,[7]
its   For summer and his° pleasures wait on thee,[8]
And thou away, the very birds are mute.[9]   12
        Or if they sing, 'tis with so dull a cheer[10]
approach   That leaves look pale, dreading the winter's near.°

1   *proud-pied*

    Splendidly dressed in many colors

2   *That heavy Saturn*

    **So that even the melancholy god
    Saturn**

3   *nor the lays*

    Neither the songs

4   *different flowers*

    Flowers differing in

5   *Could make me any summer's story tell*

    Could inspire me to tell a happy tale

6   *their proud lap*

    **I.e., the earth (which is *proud* in the
    sense of "splendid" or "showy,"
    decorated with the flowers that
    grow in it, and perhaps also *proud*
    in its more familiar sense because
    of them)**

7   *They were but sweet, but figures of delight*

    **They were merely pleasant, only
    emblems of real delight**

8   *Drawn after you, you pattern of all those*

    **Drawn in your likeness, you the
    pattern for all of them.**

98

From you have I been absent in the spring,

finery   When proud-pied[1] April, dressed in all his trim,°

Hath put a spirit of youth in everything,

That heavy Saturn[2] laughed and leapt with him.   4

neither   Yet nor° the lays[3] of birds nor the sweet smell

Of different flowers[4] in odor and in hue

Could make me any summer's story tell,[5]

Or from their proud lap[6] pluck them where they grew.   8

look with amazement   Nor did I wonder° at the lily's white,

scarlet   Nor praise the deep vermilion° in the rose;

They were but sweet, but figures of delight,[7]

Drawn after you, you pattern of all those.[8]   12

being away   Yet seemed it winter still, and, you away,°

i.e., the flowers   As with your shadow I with these° did play.

1   *Sweet thief*

     **(1) Sweet-smelling thief; (2) kind
     thief**

2   *Which on thy soft cheek for complexion
     dwells, / In my love's veins thou hast too
     grossly dyed*

     **Which for added color on your soft
     petals, you have too obviously
     dipped yourself in my beloved's
     veins. (*Purple*, in Shakespeare's
     time, covered a spectrum of red-
     dish hues.)**

3   *The lily I condemnèd for thy hand*

     **I condemned the lily for stealing its
     white color from your hand.**

4   *marjoram*

     **A fragrant and golden-brown (pre-
     sumably like the youth's hair) herb**

5   *on thorns did stand*

     **I.e., anxiously awaited their ac-
     cusation ("To be on thorns" was
     proverbially to be anxious, like our
     "on pins and needles")**

6   *had stol'n of both*

     I.e., was pink

7   *And to his robb'ry had annexed thy breath*

     **And in addition to stealing the color
     had stolen your sweet breath**

8   *in pride of all his growth*

     In his prime

9   *But sweet or color it had stol'n from thee*

     **Except ones that had stolen their
     fragrance or color from you. (This
     sonnet has fifteen lines; the first is
     introductory.)**

99

The forward° violet thus did I chide:

early blooming; bold

"Sweet thief,[1] whence didst thou steal thy sweet° that smells,

scent

If not from my love's breath? The purple pride,°

splendor

Which on thy soft cheek for complexion dwells,   4

In my love's veins thou hast too grossly dyed."[2]

The lily I condemnèd for thy hand,[3]

And buds of marjoram[4] had stol'n thy hair;

The roses fearfully on thorns did stand,[5]   8

One blushing shame, another white despair,

A third, nor° red nor white, had stol'n of both,[6]

neither

And to his robb'ry had annexed thy breath;[7]

But for his theft, in pride of all his growth[8]   12

A vengeful canker° ate him up to death.

cankerworm

More flowers I noted, yet I none could see

But sweet or color it had stol'n from thee.[9]

1 *Spend'st thou thy fury on some worthless song, / Dark'ning thy pow'r to lend base subjects light?*

   Are you using up all your passionate inspiration on some trivial verse, debasing your talents by exalting worthless individuals

2 *straight redeem / In gentle numbers time so idly spent*

   Immediately, make up for the wasted time with noble verses

3 *the ear that doth thy lays esteem / And gives thy pen both skill and argument*

   The one (i.e., my beloved) who values your songs, and gives you both the ability to write and a subject to write about

4 *If any, be a satire to decay*

   If there are any (wrinkles), be a satirist mocking the destructive action of time.

5 *time's spoils*

   Time's victories

6 *So thou prevent'st his scythe and crooked knife*

   In doing so (i.e., in giving my love fame) you defeat time's power over life. (The *scythe and crooked knife* both refer to the sickle that traditionally accompanies personified Time.)

100

Where art thou, muse, that thou forget'st so long
To speak of that which gives thee all thy might?
Spend'st thou thy fury on some worthless song,
Dark'ning thy pow'r to lend base subjects light?[1]   4
Return, forgetful muse, and straight redeem
In gentle numbers time so idly spent;[2]
Sing to the ear that doth thy lays esteem
And gives thy pen both skill and argument.[3]   8
lazy / examine   Rise, resty° muse; my love's sweet face survey°
To see if / engraved   If° time have any wrinkle graven° there;
If any, be a satire to decay,[4]
And make time's spoils[5] despisèd everywhere.   12
    Give my love fame faster than time wastes life;
    So thou prevent'st his scythe and crooked knife.[6]

1   *what shall be thy amends*

     How will you redeem yourself?

2   *in beauty dyed*

     That is suffused with beauty

3   *on my love depends*

     **(1) Need my beloved to exist; (2) rely
     on my affection**

4   *therein dignified*

     **In that dependence are you
     ennobled**

5   *Truth needs no color with his color fixed*

     **Truth requires no ornament added
     to its natural beauty.**

6   *Beauty no pencil, beauty's truth to lay*

     **Beauty needs no artist's brush to
     set out its nature.**

7   *But best is best if never intermixed*

     **The best things are best left unadul-
     terated.**

8   *To make him much outlive a gilded tomb*

     **To ensure he survives longer than a
     gold-colored monument**

9   *long hence*

     Far in the future

101

O truant° muse, what shall be thy amends[1]
For thy neglect of truth in beauty dyed?[2]
Both truth and beauty on my love depends;[3]
So dost thou too, and therein dignified.[4]

Make answer, muse: wilt thou not haply° say
"Truth needs no color with his color fixed,[5]
Beauty no pencil, beauty's truth to lay;[6]
But best is best if never intermixed"?[7]

Because he needs no praise, wilt thou be dumb?°
Excuse not silence so, for 't lies in thee
To make him much outlive a gilded tomb,[8]
And to be praised of° ages yet to be.

Then do thy office,° muse. I teach thee how
To make him seem long hence[9] as he shows° now.

---

irresponsible; lazy — O truant°
perhaps — haply°
silent — dumb?°
by — of°
duty — office,°
looks — shows°

4

8

12

1   *though less the show appear*

    Although there are fewer outward displays of it

2   *That love is merchandized whose rich esteeming / The owner's tongue doth publish everywhere.*

    That love is cheapened (by converting it to a commodity), whose value the owner publicly advertises.

3   *greet it with my lays*

    Welcome it with my poems

4   *As Philomel in summer's front doth sing*

    As the nightingale sings at the beginning of summer. (In Ovid, the princess Philomela was turned into a nightingale after her brother-in-law raped her and cut out her tongue.)

5   *stops his pipe in growth of riper days*

    I.e., stops singing as summer turns to autumn

6   *burdens every bough*

    Weighs down every branch (with common songbirds). "Burden" also is a musical term for a song's refrain.

7   *sweets grown common lose their dear delight*

    Pleasurable things that become overly familiar lose their ability to delight.

8   *dull you*

    (1) Bore you; (2) make you less special (by repeating your praises too many times)

102

My love is strengthened, though more weak in

appearance   seeming;°

I love not less, though less the show appear.[1]

That love is merchandized whose rich esteeming

The owner's tongue doth publish everywhere.[2]   4

only   Our love was new, and then but° in the spring,

accustomed   When I was wont° to greet it with my lays,[3]

As Philomel in summer's front doth sing,[4]

its   And stops his° pipe in growth of riper days.[5]   8

Not that the summer is less pleasant now

Than when her mournful hymns did hush the night,

But because   But° that wild music burdens every bough,[6]

And sweets grown common lose their dear delight.[7]   12

sometimes   Therefore, like her, I sometime° hold my tongue,

Because I would not dull you[8] with my song.

1   *poverty*

     Poor production, i.e., unsatisfac-
     tory poetry

2   *to show her pride*

     (1) To demonstrate her impressive
     talent; (2) to show off the thing she
     is proud of

3   *beside*

     (1) Added to it; (2) next to it

4   *overgoes my blunt invention quite*

     Surpasses my dulled power of
     creativity

5   *To mar the subject that before was well*

     To spoil the subject matter that was
     perfect on its own

6   *For to no other pass my verses tend*

     Because my poetry has no other
     end

7   *sit*

     (1) Be incorporated; (2) be en-
     throned

8   *shows you*

     (1) Reveals you to be; (2) reveals to
     you

103

Alack,° what poverty[1] my muse brings forth,
That, having such a scope° to show her pride,[2]
The argument° all bare° is of more worth
Than when it hath my added praise beside.[3]   4
Oh, blame me not if I no more can write.
Look in your glass,° and there appears a face
That overgoes my blunt invention quite,[4]
Dulling my lines and doing me disgrace.   8
Were it not sinful then, striving to mend,°
To mar the subject that before was well?[5]
For to no other pass my verses tend[6]
Than of your graces and your gifts to tell;   12
  And more, much more, than in my verse can sit[7]
  Your own glass shows you[8] when you look in it.

Alas
opportunity
topic / unadorned
mirror
improve on it

235

1   *your eye I eyed*

     I.e., I saw you.

2   *three summers' pride*

     Three summer's worth of splendor (i.e., leaves)

3   *Since first I saw you fresh, which yet are green*

     Since I first saw you young, who are still in your prime.

4   *yet doth beauty, like a dial hand, / Steal from his figure, and no pace perceived*

     Nonetheless beauty abandons (*doth . . . steal*) its physical appearance, as imperceptibly as the movement of the *hand* of a clock)

5   *still doth stand*

     (1) Remains unchanged; (2) shows no movement

6   *thou age unbred*

     You of generations yet unborn

7   *Ere you were born was beauty's summer dead*

     Before you were ever born the peak of beauty had already passed.

104

To me, fair friend, you never can be old,
For as you were when first your eye I eyed,[1]
Such seems your beauty still. Three winters cold
Have from the forests shook three summers' pride;[2]   4
Three beauteous springs to yellow autumn turned
progression In process° of the seasons have I seen;
Three April perfumes in three hot Junes burned,
Since first I saw you fresh, which yet are green.[3]   8
Ah, yet doth beauty, like a dial hand,
Steal from his figure, and no pace perceived;[4]
complexion So your sweet hue,° which methinks still doth stand,[5]
Hath motion, and mine eye may be deceived.   12
i.e., such deception For fear of which,° hear this, thou age unbred:[6]
Ere you were born was beauty's summer dead.[7]

1   *Still constant*

    (1) Ever faithful; (2) always the same

2   *to constancy confined*

    Limited only to the subject of
    constancy

3   *leaves out difference*

    (1) Ignores any other subject; (2)
    omits mention of disagreements

4   *spent*

    (1) Exhausted; (2) employed

5   *wondrous scope afffords*

    Offers extraordinary opportunities
    (for poetic experimentation)

6   *kept seat in one*

    Resided in the same person

105

Let not my love be called idolatry,
Nor my belovèd as an idol show,°   *be depicted*
Since all alike my songs and praises be
To one, of one, still° such, and ever so.   *constantly*   4
Kind is my love today, tomorrow kind,
Still constant[1] in a wondrous excellence;
Therefore my verse to constancy confined,[2]
One thing expressing, leaves out difference.[3]   8
Fair, kind, and true is all my argument,°   *subject matter*
Fair, kind, and true, varying to° other words;   *only with regard to*
And in this change is my invention° spent,[4]   *creativity*
Three themes in one, which wondrous scope affords.[5]   12
  Fair, kind, and true have often lived alone,°   *independently*
  Which three, till now, never kept seat in one.[6]

1   *chronicle of wasted time*

     Accounts of time past

2   *And beauty making beautiful old rhyme*

     **And their beauty lending itself to
     the old-fashioned poetry (in which
     it is depicted)**

3   *blazon*

     **A poetic convention enumerating
     each praiseworthy attribute of the
     subject**

4   *would have expressed / Even such a
     beauty as you master now*

     **Was attempting to describe the
     kind of beauty you now possess**

5   *So all their praises are but prophecies*

     **As such, everything they wrote was
     merely a prediction**

6   *all you prefiguring*

     All anticipating your image

7   *but with divining eyes*

     **Only with eyes that predict the
     future**

8   *Have eyes to wonder, but lack tongues to
     praise*

     **Have eyes to marvel at you, but
     lack the ability to celebrate you
     appropriately**

106

When in the chronicle of wasted time [1]
people   I see descriptions of the fairest wights,°
And beauty making beautiful old rhyme [2]
In praise of ladies dead and lovely knights,   4
Then in the blazon [3] of sweet beauty's best,
Of hand, of foot, of lip, of eye, of brow,
I see their antique pen would have expressed
Even such a beauty as you master now. [4]   8
So all their praises are but prophecies [5]
Of this our time, all you prefiguring; [6]
because   And, for° they looked but with divining eyes, [7]
They had not skill enough your worth to sing;   12
Because even   For° we which now behold these present days,
Have eyes to wonder, but lack tongues to praise. [8]

1   *prophetic soul*

Speculative imagination

2   *the lease of my true love control*

**Set a limit to the allotted time I have
to love you**

3   *Supposed as forfeit to a confined doom*

**Thought to expire after a limited
period of time**

4   *The mortal moon hath her eclipse endured*

**A tantalizing phrase that scholars
have variously identified, sometimes with the defeat of the Spanish
armada (1588), which attacked in
a crescent formation; sometimes
with Queen Elizabeth I herself, who
was associated with Diana, the
moon goddess, and was rumored
to have survived a serious illness
in 1599; and sometimes with the
peaceful accession of King James
I after Elizabeth's death in 1603. In
the absence of any certain chronol-
ogy for the writing of the sonnets,
scholars have attempted to date
Sonnet 107 on the basis of this
ambiguous allusion.**

5   *sad augurs mock their own presage*

**Pessimistic prophets now make fun
of their own predictions.**

6   *Incertainties now crown themselves
assured*

**Events once anxiously anticipated
are now happily settled.**

7   *peace proclaims olives of endless age*

**These quiet times promise an
enduring time of peace. (The olive
and the olive branch are traditional
symbols of peace.)**

8   *with the drops of this most balmy time*

**I.e., with the wholesome effects of
the propitious times we live in**

9   *Death to me subscribes*

Death submits to my power.

10 *While he insults o'er dull and speechless
tribes*

**While he gloats in triumph over
those people who do not have
poetry to keep them alive**

11 *tyrants' crests*

The coats of arms of tyrants

107

Not° mine own fears nor the prophetic soul [1]   *Neither*
Of the wide world dreaming on° things to come   *about*
Can yet the lease of my true love control, [2]
Supposed as forfeit to a confined doom. [3]   4
The mortal moon hath her eclipse endured [4]
And the sad augurs mock their own presage. [5]
Incertainties now crown themselves assured, [6]
And peace proclaims olives of endless age. [7]   8
Now with the drops of this most balmy time [8]
My love looks fresh, and Death to me subscribes, [9]
Since, spite of him, I'll live in this poor rhyme,
While he insults o'er dull and speechless tribes. [10]   12
And thou in this° shalt find thy monument,   *i.e., this poem*
When tyrants' crests [11] and tombs of brass are spent.°   *worn away*

1   *What's in the brain that ink may character*

    What thoughts are there that can be written down?

2   *What's new to speak, what now to register*

    What new phrase can be invented, what is still unrecorded

3   *Counting no old thing old*

    Not considering any well-worn phrase to be outdated

4   *hallowed*

    (1) Made holy; (2) called out

5   *in love's fresh case*

    Expressed in terms that never lose their vitality

6   *Weighs not the dust and injury of age*

    Takes no account of the degrading effects of time

7   *Nor gives to necessary wrinkles place*

    Nor pays attention to the inevitable *wrinkles*

8   *But makes antiquity for aye his page*

    But rather makes old age his servant forever

9   *the first conceit of love there bred*

    Love as it was first experienced still being generated

108

What's in the brain that ink may character[1]
depicted   Which hath not figured° to thee my true spirit?
What's new to speak, what now to register,[2]
precious   That may express my love or thy dear° merit?   4
Nothing, sweet boy; but yet, like prayers divine,
I must each day say o'er the very same,
Counting no old thing old,[3] thou mine, I thine,
Even as when first I hallowed[4] thy fair name.   8
So that eternal love in love's fresh case[5]
Weighs not the dust and injury of age,[6]
Nor gives to necessary wrinkles place,[7]
But makes antiquity for aye his page,[8]   12
  Finding the first conceit of love there bred,[9]
obsolete   Where time and outward form would show it dead.°

1   *Though absence seemed my flame to
    qualify*

    **Though my absence seemed to
    lessen my passion**

2   *As easy might I from my self depart / As
    from my soul, which in thy breast doth lie.*

    **I could as easily be separated from
    my being as from my spirit, which
    lives in your heart.**

3   *Just to the time, not with the time
    exchanged*

    **Right on time, unchanged in (or
    "by") the time that has passed**

4   *for my stain*

    **For washing away my transgression
    (with my tears).**

5   *All frailties that besiege all kinds of blood*

    **Each of the moral failings that
    weaken every temperament**

6   *That it could so preposterously be stained*

    **That it (i.e., my nature) could so
    absurdly be corrupted**

7   *To leave for nothing all thy sum of good*

    **To leave all your good qualities (1)
    for no reason; (2) in exchange for
    nothing**

8   *For nothing this wide universe I call, /
    Save thou*

    **I consider the whole universe to be
    nothing, except for you.**

109

Oh, never say that I was false of heart,
Though absence seemed my flame to qualify.[1]
As easy might I from my self depart
As from my soul, which in thy breast doth lie.[2]   4

roamed   That is my home of love; if I have ranged,°

one   Like him° that travels I return again,
Just to the time, not with the time exchanged,[3]
So that myself bring water for my stain.[4]   8
Never believe, though in my nature reigned
All frailties that besiege all kinds of blood,[5]
That it could so preposterously be stained,[6]
To leave for nothing all thy sum of good.[7]   12
  For nothing this wide universe I call,
  Save thou,[8] my rose; in it thou art my all.

1   *And made myself a motley to the view*

   And made myself a fool in the eyes of the world

2   *Gored*

   (1) Dishonored; (2) wounded; (3) sullied

3   *Made old offenses of affections new*

   Committed old crimes with new love objects

4   *truth*

   (1) Fidelity; (2) true love; (3) honesty

5   *Askance and strangely*

   Disdainfully and as if *truth* were a stranger to me

6   *blenches*

   (1) Swervings; (2) blemishes, flaws; (3) indirect glances

7   *another youth*

   (1) Renewed youth; (2) another young man

8   *And worse essays proved thee my best of love*

   And experiencing lesser loves proved you are the best love

9   *all is done*

   All of that is finished.

10 *will grind / On newer proof*

   Will sharpen (as in grinding a blade against a stone) by experimenting with new people

11 *to try*

   (1) Put to the test; (2) subject to a trying experience

12 *I am confined*

   (1) I limit myself; (2) I am imprisoned

13 *next my Heaven the best*

   I.e., you who are the next best thing to Heaven

110

Alas 'tis true, I have gone here and there,
And made myself a motley to the view,[1]
Gored[2] mine own thoughts, sold cheap what is most
valuable dear,°
Made old offenses of affections new.[3]   4
Most true it is that I have looked on truth[4]
Askance and strangely;[5] but, by all above,
These blenches[6] gave my heart another youth,[7]
And worse essays proved thee my best of love.[8]   8
Now all is done,[9] save what shall have no end;
Mine appetite I never more will grind
On newer proof,[10] to try[11] an older friend,
A god in love, to whom I am confined.[12]   12
  Then give me welcome, next my Heaven the best,[13]
  Even to thy pure and most most loving breast.

1   *The guilty goddess of my harmful deeds*

    The goddess who is responsible for my misdeeds

2   *Than public means which public manners breeds*

    Than depending on the public (as a commercial playwright?), which causes me to behave like them

3   *Thence comes it that my name receives a brand*

    As a result my reputation is disgraced. (Criminals in early modern England were branded for certain crimes.)

4   *And almost thence my nature is subdued / To what it works in, like the dyer's hand*

    And for that reason *my nature* is almost overcome by the environment in which it works, as a *dyer's hand* is stained by the dyes he works with.

5   *renewed*

    Restored to what I was before

6   *eisel*

    A sour vinegar used as medicine

7   *Nor double penance to correct correction*

    Nor will I think it a double penalty to correct what has already been corrected

8   *Even that your pity*

    That your very pity

111

Oh, for my sake do you with Fortune chide,° *dispute*
The guilty goddess of my harmful deeds,[1]
That did not better for my life° provide *livelihood*
Than public means which public manners breeds.[2]   4
Thence comes it that my name receives a brand,[3]
And almost thence my nature is subdued
To what it works in, like the dyer's hand.[4]
Pity me then, and wish I were renewed,[5]   8
Whilst like a willing patient I will drink
Potions of eisel[6] 'gainst my strong infection.
No° bitterness that I will bitter think, *There is no*
Nor double penance to correct correction.[7]   12
  Pity me then, dear friend, and I assure ye,
  Even that your pity[8] is enough to cure me.

1   *doth th' impression fill / Which vulgar scandal stamped upon my brow*

    Heal the wound that public disgrace inflicted on my face

2   *For what care I who calls me well or ill, / So you o'er-green my bad, my good allow*

    What do I care what people say about me as long as you forgive my wrongs and recognize my good deeds?

3   *None else to me, nor I to none, alive, / That my steeled sense o'erchanges right or wrong*

    There is no one else important enough to me, or to whom I am sufficiently important, so that my fixed opinion of what is *right or wrong* is overturned.

4   *so profound abysm*

    Such a deep pit

5   *my adder's sense / To critic and to flatter stoppèd are*

    I am deaf to criticism and flattery. (Adders were proverbially able to close their ears.)

6   *with my neglect I do dispense*

    I justify my indifference (to everyone else)

7   *You are so strongly in my purpose bred / That all the world besides me thinks you're dead*

    You are so powerfully brought into being by my (poetic) activities that everyone except me thinks you must be dead.

112

Your love and pity doth th' impression fill
Which vulgar scandal stamped upon my brow,[1]
For what care I who calls me well or ill,
So you o'er-green my bad, my good allow?[2]   4
You are my all-the-world, and I must strive
To know my shames and praises from your tongue;
None else to me, nor I to none, alive,
That my steeled sense o'erchanges right or wrong.[3] 8
In so profound abysm[4] I throw all care
Of others' voices, that my adder's sense
To critic and to flatterer stoppèd are.[5]

Notice Mark° how with my neglect I do dispense:[6]   12
        You are so strongly in my purpose bred[7]
        That all the world besides me thinks you're dead.

1   *that which governs me to go about*

That which allows me to get around (i.e., my sight)

2   *Doth part his function*

Partly functions

3   *is out*

Is put out or extinguished

4   *For it no form delivers to the heart*

Because (my eyesight) sends no images to my heart

5   *Of his quick objects hath the mind no part*

Of the fleeting things the eyes see, the mind apprehends nothing.

6   *Nor his own vision holds what it doth catch*

Nor does the eye retain any image of what it momentarily catches sight of

7   *rud'st or gentlest*

Crudest or most noble

8   *it shapes them to your feature*

It transforms them into images of you.

9   *Incapable of more, replete with you*

Unable to take in more, filled up by you

10   *My most true mind thus mak'th mine eye untrue*

My mind is so faithfully committed to you that it makes my vision unreliable.

113

Since I left you, mine eye is in my mind,
And that which governs me to go about[1]
Doth part his function,[2] and is partly blind,
Seems° seeing, but effectually is out;[3]   4
  i.e., Seems to be

For it no form delivers to the heart[4]
Of bird, of flow'r, or shape which it doth latch.°
  catch sight of

Of his quick objects hath the mind no part,[5]
Nor his own vision holds what it doth catch;[6]   8
For if it see the rud'st or gentlest[7] sight,
The most sweet favor or deformèd'st creature,
The mountain or the sea, the day or night,
The crow or dove, it shapes them to your feature.[8]   12
  Incapable of more, replete with you,[9]
  My most true mind thus mak'th mine eye untrue.[10]

1   *Or whether*

Here and in line 3 the phrase introduces alternative possibilities. In modern English, we would have only the *or* in line 3.

2   *doth my mind, being crowned with you*

Is it that my mind, honored by your love

3   *your love taught it this alchemy*

I.e., my love for you, taught my eye *alchemy*—the power to transform common objects into precious things.

4   *To make of monsters and things indigest / Such cherubins as your sweet self resemble*

To construct out of grotesque creatures and shapeless forms angelic beings that look like you

5   *Creating every bad a perfect best / As fast as objects to his beams assemble*

Making every bad thing into a flawless one, as soon as objects take shape in his sight

6   *'tis the first; 'tis flatt'ry in my seeing*

It is the first suggestion: it's my delusional eyesight.

7   *most kingly*

Like a king, i.e., enjoying the *flattery* (see line 2)

8   *to his palate doth prepare the cup*

To please his taste prepares the drink

9   *If it be poisoned, 'tis the lesser sin / That mine eye loves it and doth first begin.*

I.e., even if the false flattery corrupts, it will not be so bad because my eye, which approves the flattery, drinks first. (The conceit likens the eye to a king's taster, who risks swallowing the poison intended for the king.)

114

Or whether[1] doth my mind, being crowned with you,[2]
Drink up the monarch's plague, this flattery,
Or whether shall I say mine eye saith true,
And that your love taught it this alchemy,[3]   4
To make of monsters and things indigest
Such cherubins as your sweet self resemble,[4]
Creating every bad a perfect best
As fast as objects to his beams assemble?[5]   8
Oh, 'tis the first; 'tis flatt'ry in my seeing,[6]

pompous And my great° mind most kingly[7] drinks it up.

aste; appetite / agreeing Mine eye well knows what with his gust° is 'greeing,°
And to his palate doth prepare the cup.[8]   12
  If it be poisoned, 'tis the lesser sin
   That mine eye loves it and doth first begin.[9]

1   *My most full flame*

   I.e., the height of my passion

2   *But reckoning time,*

   **(1) But taking time into consider-
ation; (2) but time, which takes
its toll**

3   *millioned accidents*

   Millions of unforeseen events

4   *Creep in 'twixt vows*

   **Sneak in between promises and
their fulfillment**

5   *Divert strong minds to th' course of
alt'ring things*

   **Lead confident people to change
their minds**

6   *Might I not then say*

   Could I not have said at that time

7   *certain o'er incertainty*

   Certain beyond any uncertainty

8   *Crowning the present*

   Revelling in my present happiness

9   *Love is a babe*

   Love (like Cupid) is just a baby.

10 *say so*

   I.e., say "Now I love you best"

11 *To give full growth to that which still doth
grow*

   **I.e., to imply (by saying "best") that
my love is fully developed instead
of still increasing**

115

Those lines that I before have writ do lie,

Precisely   Even° those that said I could not love you dearer;

However; As yet   Yet° then my judgment knew no reason why

My most full flame[1] should afterwards burn clearer.   4

But reckoning time,[2] whose millioned accidents[3]

Creep in 'twixt vows,[4] and change decrees of kings,

Darken / intentions   Tan° sacred beauty, blunt the sharp'st intents,°

Divert strong minds to th' course of alt'ring things.[5]   8

Alas, why, fearing of time's tyranny,

Might I not then say,[6] "Now I love you best,"

When I was certain o'er incertainty,[7]

anxious   Crowning the present,[8] doubting° of the rest?   12

Love is a babe;[9] then might I not say so,[10]

To give full growth to that which still doth grow?[11]

1   *Let me not*

(1) May I never; (2) do not allow
me to

2   *Admit impediments*

(1) Concede that there might be
obstacles; (2) permit the consideration of obstacles. (In the
Elizabethan marriage ceremony,
the couple was asked "if either of
you do know any *impediment* why ye
may not be lawfully joined together
in matrimony.")

3   *bends with the remover to remove*

Turns away (i.e., stops loving) when
the loved one leaves (or dies)

4   *an ever-fixèd mark*

An eternally unmoving point of
reference (like a lighthouse or
beacon at sea)

5   *the star to every wand'ring bark,*

The guiding star (like the North
Star) for every ship at sea.

6   *Whose worth's unknown, although his
height be taken*

The value of which (i.e., the star's)
cannot be known, even though its
height (over the horizon) can be
calculated.

7   *But bears it out even to the edge of doom*

But endures even to the very end of
time (i.e., Judgment Day)

8   *If this be error and upon me proved, / I
never writ, nor no man ever loved.*

If this belief is wrong, and is proved
against me as such, then I never
wrote anything and no man was
ever in love (or, I never loved any
man).

116

Let me not[1] to the marriage of true minds
Admit impediments;[2] love is not love
Which alters when it alteration finds,
Or bends with the remover to remove.[3]   4
Oh, no, it is an ever-fixèd mark[4]
That looks on tempests and is never shaken;
It is the star to every wand'ring bark,[5]
Whose worth's unknown, although his height be
    taken.[6]   8
Love's not Time's fool, though rosy lips and cheeks
its Within his° bending sickle's compass come.
Love alters not with his brief hours and weeks,
But bears it out even to the edge of doom.[7]   12
  If this be error and upon me proved,
  I never writ, nor no man ever loved.[8]

1   *upon your dearest love to call*

    (1) To avail myself of your love; (2) to plead for your love; (3) to visit you

2   *Whereto all bonds*

    To which all obligations (both moral and emotional)

3   *frequent been with unknown minds*

    Often spent my time with strangers

4   *given to time your own dear-purchased right*

    Frittered away the time that rightfully belonged to you

5   *That I have hoisted sail to all the winds / Which should transport me farthest from your sight*

    I.e., I have followed every whim that might take me away from you.

6   *willfulness*

    Deliberate selfishness (as opposed to the unintended *errors* he has also committed)

7   *on just proof surmise accumulate*

    Add to the evidence you have (of my wrongdoings) your suspicions (about what else I have done)

8   *within the level*

    In range; in the line of fire

9   *Since my appeal says I did strive to prove / The constancy and virtue of your love*

    Because in my defense I argue that I was trying to test how constant and virtuous your love is (by seeing if you would forgive me)

117

Accuse me thus: that I have scanted° all   *stinted on*
Wherein° I should your great deserts repay,   *With which*
Forgot upon your dearest love to call,[1]
Whereto all bonds[2] do tie me day by day;   4
That I have frequent been with unknown minds,[3]
And given to time your own dear-purchased right;[4]
That I have hoisted sail to all the winds
Which should transport me farthest from your sight.[5]   8
Book° both my willfulness[6] and errors down,   *Write*
And on just proof surmise accumulate.[7]
Bring me within the level[8] of your frown,
But shoot not at me in your wakened° hate,   *newly aroused*   12
    Since my appeal says I did strive to prove
    The constancy and virtue of your love.[9]

1   *eager compounds*

Highly seasoned concoctions (the
bitter sauces of line 6)

2   *We sicken to shun sickness when we purge*

We make ourselves sick to avoid
getting sick. (In Shakespeare's
day it was common to periodically
***purge*, or induce vomiting, which**
was believed to prevent illness.)

3   *ne'er-cloying*

Never too sweet

4   *I frame my feeding*

I modified my diet (i.e., altered the
company I keep).

5   *a kind of meetness / To be diseased ere*
     that there was true needing

Some sort of appropriateness in
being sick before there was a real
cause for it

6   *grew to faults assured*

Turned into actual disorders

7   *brought to medicine*

Caused to require *medicine*

8   *rank of*

With excess of

9   *so fell sick of you*

(1) Fell so very sick on account of
you; (2) in this manner grew tired
of you

118

Like° as to make our appetites more keen   *Just*
With eager compounds[1] we our palate urge,°   *stimulate*
As,° to prevent our maladies unseen,   *Just as*
We sicken to shun sickness when we purge;[2]   4
Even so, being full of your ne'er-cloying[3] sweetness,
To bitter sauces did I frame my feeding,[4]
And, sick of welfare,° found a kind of meetness   *good health*
To be diseased ere that there was true needing.[5]   8
Thus policy° in love, t' anticipate°   *cunning/forestall*
The ills that were not, grew to faults assured,[6]
And brought to medicine[7] a healthful state
Which, rank of[8] goodness, would by ill be cured;   12
But thence° I learn, and find the lesson true: *from this*
Drugs poison him that so fell sick of you.[9]

1   *siren tears*

Tempting, yet deceptive tears. (In
Greek myth, Sirens were half-
woman, half-bird creatures who,
with their singing, lured sailors to
their deaths.)

2   *limbecks*

Vessels for distillation; stills for
making liquor

3   *I saw myself to win*

Losing my fight (against my
sickness) just as I thought I had
overcome it

4   *so blessèd never*

Never more fortunate than at that
moment

5   *out of their spheres been fitted*

I.e., bulged out (literally, been
forced out of their sockets)

6   *benefit of ill*

The advantage of sickness

7   *That better is by evil still made better*

I.e., good things are improved if
they have to overcome evil (as in
the commonplace idea that broken
bones heal stronger than they were
before).

8   *So I return, rebuked, to my content*

Therefore, having learned the error
of my ways, I come back to what
makes me happy.

119

What potions have I drunk of siren tears [1]
Distilled from limbecks [2] foul as hell within,
Administering   Applying° fears to hopes and hopes to fears,
Nonetheless   Still° losing when I saw myself to win! [3]   4
What wretched errors hath my heart committed,
Whilst it hath thought itself so blessèd never! [4]
How have mine eyes out of their spheres been fitted [5]
temporary madness   In the distraction° of this madding fever!   8
Oh, benefit of ill! [6] Now I find true
That better is by evil still made better, [7]
And ruined love when it is built anew
Grows fairer than at first, more strong, far greater.   12
   So I return, rebuked, to my content, [8]
   And gain by ills thrice more than I have spent.

1   *Needs must I under my transgression bow*
     I must now repent my offense.

2   *a hell of time*
     A hellishly painful period

3   *our night of woe*
     The dark time of our sadness

4   *My deepest sense*
     The depths of my feeling

5   *soon to you, as you to me, then tend'red /*
     The humble salve which wounded bosoms
     fits
     Offered you, as quickly as you of-
     fered me, the simple medicine that
     cures a broken heart

6   *Mine ransoms yours, and yours must*
     ransom me
     I.e., my trespass pardons yours, and
     your crime must excuse mine.

120

That you were once unkind befriends° me now, — *gives me comfort*

And for° that sorrow which I then did feel — *on account of*

Needs must I under my transgression bow,[1]

Unless my nerves° were brass or hammered steel. — *sinews*   4

For if you were by my unkindness shaken,

As I by yours, you've passed a hell of time,[2]

And I, a tyrant, have no leisure° taken — *opportunity*

To weigh° how once I suffered in° your crime. — *consider / from*   8

Oh, that our night of woe[3] might have rememb'red° — *reminded; recalled to*

My deepest sense,[4] how hard true sorrow hits,

And soon to you, as you to me, then tend'red

The humble salve which wounded bosoms fits![5]   12

   But that your trespass° now becomes a fee;° — *offense / payment*

   Mine ransoms yours, and yours must ransom me.[6]

1   *so deemed*

     I.e., judged to be vile

2   *by others' seeing*

     (1) According to the judgment of
     others; (2) because others are aware
     of it

3   *Give salutation to my sportive blood*

     Acknowledge my wanton
     tendencies

4   *on my frailties why are frailer spies*

     Why do people even more flawed
     than I am worry about my failures?

5   *Which in their wills count bad*

     Who are determined to think im-
     moral

6   *bevel*

     Literally, zigzag or crooked, a geo-
     metric metaphor for dishonest, as
     straight is for honest

7   *By their rank thoughts my deeds must not
     be shown*

     My actions should not be judged
     according to their corrupt
     opinions.

8   *in their badness reign*

     Prosper because they take
     advantage of their *badness*

121

'Tis better to be vile than vile esteemed,
i.e., be vile When not to be° receives reproach of being,
legitimate And the just° pleasure lost which is so deemed [1]
Not by our feeling but by others' seeing. [2]   4
corrupted; adulterous For why should others' false adulterate° eyes
Give salutation to my sportive blood? [3]
Or on my frailties why are frailer spies, [4]
Which in their wills count bad [5] what I think good?   8
aim No, I am that I am, and they that level°
misdeeds / count At my abuses° reckon° up their own.
honest I may be straight,° though they themselves be bevel; [6]
By their rank thoughts my deeds must not be shown, [7]   12
universal / assert Unless this general° evil they maintain:°
All men are bad, and in their badness reign. [8]

1   *Thy gift, thy tables*

     **The notebooks you gave me (see
     also LONGER NOTE on page 364)**

2   *Full charactered*

     Completely written in

3   *Which shall above that idle rank remain*

     **(My memory) will last longer than
     (or remain superior to) the insig-
     nificant letters on the page.**

4   *Beyond all date*

     Past all limits of time

5   *Have faculty by nature to subsist*

     **Are allowed *by nature* the ability to
     survive**

6   *Till each to razed oblivion yield his part /
     Of thee*

     **I.e., until the brain and heart sur-
     render to obliterating forgetful-
     ness the features of you that they
     hold**

7   *thy record never can be missed*

     The memory of you cannot be lost.

8   *poor retention*

     **Inadequate preserver (i.e., the
     notebooks, or *tables*, in line 1).**

9   *Nor need I tallies thy dear love to score*

     **Nor do I need to keep track of your
     love by making notches on a stick**

10   *to give them from me was I bold / To trust
     those tables that receive thee more*

     **I dared to give away (the notebooks
     you gave me) so that I might rely
     on the tables of my memory that
     preserve you better.**

11   *keep an adjunct*

     **Employ an assistant, or outside aid
     (i.e., the notebooks)**

12   *Were to import*

     **(1) Would imply; (2) Would be to
     introduce**

122

Thy gift, thy tables,[1] are within my brain
Full charactered[2] with lasting memory,
Which shall above that idle rank remain[3]
Beyond all date,[4] even to eternity—   4
Or, at the least, so long as brain and heart
Have faculty by nature to subsist[5]—
Till each to razed oblivion yield his part
Of thee,[6] thy record never can be missed.[7]   8
That poor retention[8] could not so much hold,
Nor need I tallies thy dear love to score;[9]
Therefore to give them from me was I bold
To trust those tables that receive thee more.[10]   12
  To keep an adjunct[11] to remember thee
  Were to import[12] forgetfulness in me.

1   *pyramids*

    Probably refers to obelisks rather
    than the pyramids of Egypt, yet
    here symbolizing any massive man-
    made structure or monument

2   *built up with newer might*

    Recently constructed (as opposed
    to the ancient pyramids)

3   *nothing novel, nothing strange*

    Not anything new or astonishing

4   *dressings of a former sight*

    New versions of things that have
    been seen before

5   *Our dates are brief*

    The time we have on earth is short.

6   *What thou dost foist upon us that is old*

    The old things you try to palm off
    on us as new

7   *rather make them born to our desire /
    Than think that we before have heard
    them told*

    Prefer to think we invented them
    rather than remember that we have
    heard about them before

8   *doth lie, / Made more or less by thy
    continual haste*

    Are deceptive, either built up or
    worn away by time's constant
    passage

9   *this shall ever be*

    (1) The idea expressed in the follow-
    ing line will be true; (2) this poem
    will always exist.

123

No! Time, thou shalt not boast that I do change.
Thy pyramids[1] built up with newer might[2]
To me are nothing novel, nothing strange;[3]
They are but dressings of a former sight.[4]   4

marvel at   Our dates are brief,[5] and therefore we admire°
What thou dost foist upon us that is old,[6]
And rather make them born to our desire
Than think that we before have heard them told.[7]   8

records; monuments   Thy registers° and thee I both defy,
marveling   Not wond'ring° at the present nor the past,
For thy records, and what we see, doth lie,
Made more or less by thy continual haste.[8]   12

  This I do vow, and this shall ever be:[9]
faithful   I will be true° despite thy scythe and thee.

1   *If my dear love were but the child of state*
    **If my precious affection were
    merely the product of circumstance**

2   *for Fortune's bastard, be unfathered*
    **Be disavowed as the bastard child
    of Fortune**

3   *As subject to time's love or to time's hate*
    **I.e., at the mercy of the fashions of
    the moment**

4   *Weeds among weeds, or flowers with
    flowers gathered*
    **Thrown in with either weeds or
    flowers (both of which are subject
    to time's effects).**

5   *far from accident*
    **Well away from the influence of
    chance**

6   *It suffers not in smiling pomp, nor falls /
    Under the blow of thrallèd discontent*
    **I.e., it does not weaken when flat-
    tered by the favor of the rich and
    powerful, nor is it lessened by the
    cynicism of the disaffected.**

7   *Whereto th' inviting time our fashion
    calls*
    **To which "favor" or "cynicism" (see
    note 6) the present age inclines us**

8   *policy, that heretic*
    **Expediency (personified as a
    scoundrel)**

9   *Which works on leases of short-numb'red
    hours*
    **Who makes only short-term
    commitments**

10 *But all alone stands hugely politic*
    **But (my love) is the only thing that is
    truly magisterial**

11 *To this I witness call the fools of time*
    **To testify to this truth I summon
    as witnesses all those fools who
    have been *subject to time's love or to
    time's hate***

12 *Which die for goodness, who have lived
    for crime*
    **The final couplet has generated
    much critical discussion, but its
    general sense is that *the fools of time*
    with their opportunistic sense of
    love provide unwitting testimony
    that the poet's love is superior to
    theirs.**

124

If my dear love were but the child of state,[1]
It might, for Fortune's bastard, be unfathered,[2]
As subject to time's love or to time's hate,[3]
Weeds among weeds, or flowers with flowers
  gathered.[4]   4

i.e., my love No, it° was builded far from accident;[5]
It suffers not in smiling pomp, nor falls
Under the blow of thrallèd discontent,[6]
Whereto th' inviting time our fashion calls.[7]   8
It fears not policy, that heretic,[8]
Which works on leases of short-numb'red hours,[9]
But all alone stands hugely politic,[10]

In that / neither That° it nor° grows with heat nor drowns with show'rs.   12
  To this I witness call the fools of time,[11]
  Which die for goodness, who have lived for crime.[12]

1   *Were 't ought to me I bore the canopy*

Would it matter to me if I carried
the canopy (of a monarch during his
coronation)

2   *the outward honoring*

Paying homage to public displays

3   *laid great bases for eternity, / Which
proves more short than waste or ruining*

I.e., built huge foundations to last
forever, which turn out to last no
longer than time's decay or destruc-
tion allow

4   *dwellers on form and favor*

Those who are only concerned with
beauty and patronage

5   *paying too much rent, / For compound
sweet forgoing simple savor*

Spending too much, and in their
sophisticated taste forgoing simple
pleasures

6   *Pitiful thrivers, in their gazing spent*

I.e., those who seek to thrive, but
are actually pathetic, ruined by
their care for *form and favor* (line 5)

7   *oblation, poor but free*

Ritual offering (i.e., my love), which
is simple but given willingly

8   *with seconds*

Inferior substances

9   *Hence, thou suborned informer!*

Go away, you perjured witness!
(This seems to be addressed to
Time, who implicitly claims the
poet is in his power, but see line 14.)

125

Were 't ought to me I bore the canopy,[1]

appearance With my extern° the outward honoring,[2]

Or laid great bases for eternity,

Which proves more short than waste or ruining?[3]   4

Have I not seen dwellers on form and favor[4]

Lose all and more by paying too much rent,

For compound sweet forgoing simple savor,[5]

Pitiful thrivers, in their gazing spent?[6]   8

devoted No, let me be obsequious° in thy heart,

And take thou my oblation, poor but free,[7]

Which is not mixed with seconds,[8] knows no art

exchange But mutual render,° only me for thee.   12

Hence, thou suborned informer![9] A true soul

accused/power When most impeached° stands least in thy control.°

1   *Dost hold Time's fickle glass*

Has control over Time's ever-
changing hourglass

2   *his sickle hour*

I.e., the moment Time swings his
sickle to cut down the living

3   *hast by waning grown*

By aging has flourished (or, grown
more beautiful)

4   *As thou goest onwards still will pluck thee
back*

As you continue to age she will continually try to hold you back (from
wrack, i.e., decay).

5   *keeps*

Cares for, holds on to (but see *keep*
in line 10)

6   *that her skill / May Time disgrace, and
wretched minutes kill*

So that her ability to ward off decay
may dishonor Time and defeat his
destructive action

7   *Her audit, though delayed, answered
must be, / And her quietus is to render
thee.*

Nature's debt, though its due date
may be postponed, must be paid
(to Time), and the ultimate settling
of her account (*quietus*) is to hand
you over (to him).

8   (   )/(   )

See Longer Note on page 364.

126

O thou, my lovely boy, who in thy power
Dost hold Time's fickle glass,[1] his sickle hour,[2]
in so doing Who hast by waning grown,[3] and therein° show'st
Thy lovers withering, as thy sweet self grow'st.   4
ruin; decay If Nature, sovereign mistress over wrack,°
As thou goest onwards still will pluck thee back,[4]
for She keeps[5] thee to° this purpose: that her skill
May Time disgrace, and wretched minutes kill.[6]   8
I.e., Nature / darling Yet fear her,° O thou minion° of her pleasure;
always She may detain, but not still° keep, her treasure.
Her audit, though delayed, answered must be,
And her quietus is to render thee.[7]   12
(   )
(   )[8]

1   *In the old age, black was not counted fair*

In the past, dark coloring was not considered beautiful. (Throughout the poem, *fair* alternates between its meanings of "beautiful" and "light in color.")

2   *Or, if it were, it bore not beauty's name*

Or if black was considered fair it was never called beautiful

3   *But now is black beauty's successive heir*

But today, dark coloring is the legitimate inheritor of the name of beauty

4   *And beauty slandered with a bastard shame*

And what was formerly considered beautiful (i.e., fair coloring) is now rejected and disgraced

5   *For since each hand hath put on nature's power*

Since every human hand has appropriated nature's prerogative (i.e., by artificially creating beauty with cosmetics)

6   *Fairing the foul with art's false borrowed face*

Making the ugly look beautiful with cosmetics

7   *hath no name, no holy bow'r*

Has no reputation, no sacred dwelling place (because false beauty has usurped beauty's name and residence)

8   *suited*

Well-suited to this age

9   *they mourners seem / At such who, not born fair, no beauty lack*

Her black eyes seem to mourn for those who, though not born beautiful, lack no beauty (because they wear makeup).

10 *Sland'ring creation with a false esteem*

I.e., their made-up faces disparaging what nature has created by the praise they get for their artificial beauty

11 *becoming of their woe, / That every tongue says beauty should look so*

Beautifully suited to their grief (see note 9 above) so that everyone now says that beauty should be dark (like *my mistress' eyes*)

127

In the old age, black was not counted fair,[1]
Or, if it were, it bore not beauty's name;[2]
But now is black beauty's successive heir,[3]
And beauty slandered with a bastard shame.[4]   4
For since each hand hath put on nature's power,[5]
Fairing the foul with art's false borrowed face,[6]
Sweet beauty hath no name, no holy bow'r,[7]
made ordinary But is profaned,° if not lives in disgrace.   8
Therefore my mistress' eyes are raven black,
Her eyes so suited,[8] and they mourners seem
At such who, not born fair, no beauty lack,[9]
Sland'ring creation with a false esteem.[10]   12
i.e., her eyes Yet so they° mourn, becoming of their woe,
That every tongue says beauty should look so.[11]

1   *thou, my music,*

     You who are music to my heart

2   *blessèd wood*

     The wood of the virginal, an instru-
     ment resembling a harpsichord,
     which is blessed by your touch

3   *The wiry concord that mine ear confounds*

     The harmony of plucked strings
     that amazes my ear

4   *jacks*

     Keys of the instrument (with a play
     on *jacks* meaning knaves or com-
     mon fellows, as also in line 13)

5   *the tender inward*

     I.e., the palm

6   *which should that harvest reap*

     Which should receive the bounty of
     your kisses

7   *To be so tickled they would change their
     state / And situation with those dancing
     chips*

     To be touched so teasingly my
     lips would gladly turn their flesh
     to wood, and switch their position
     with those keys.

128

How oft when thou, my music,[1] music play'st
Upon that blessèd wood[2] whose motion° sounds
With thy sweet fingers, when thou gently sway'st°
The wiry concord that mine ear confounds,[3]   4
Do I envy those jacks[4] that nimble leap
To kiss the tender inward[5] of thy hand,
Whilst my poor lips, which should that harvest reap,[6]
At the wood's boldness by° thee blushing stand.   8
To be so tickled they would change their state
And situation with those dancing chips,[7]
O'er whom thy fingers walk with gentle gait,
Making dead wood more blest than living lips.   12
Since saucy° jacks so happy are in this,
Give them thy fingers, me thy lips to kiss.

movement; action — line 2
rule over — line 3
near — line 8
presumptuous — line 13

1   *Th' expense of spirit in a waste of shame /*
Is lust in action

**Lust's enactment (i.e., sexual inter-
course) is the shameful squander-
ing of vital energy.**

2   *till action, lust / Is perjured*

**Until it is satisfied, lust lies to
achieve its ends.**

3   *full of blame*

Wholly culpable

4   *Past reason hunted*

Irrationally pursued

5   *in possession so*

Once gained is equally mad

6   *A bliss in proof, and proved, a very woe*

**A great pleasure in the experience,
and afterward a source of sorrow**

7   *Before, a joy proposed; behind, a dream*

**While still ahead of you, a joy in
anticipation; once over as insub-
stantial and unsatisfying as a dream**

8   *All this the world well knows, yet none
knows well / To shun the heaven that
leads men to this hell.*

**Everyone knows this already, yet no
one knows it well enough to give
up the pleasure that leads men to
this misery.**

129

Th' expense of spirit in a waste of shame
Is lust in action,[1] and, till action, lust
murderous   Is perjured,[2] murd'rous, bloody,° full of blame,[3]
to be trusted   Savage, extreme, rude, cruel, not to trust;°   4
immediately   Enjoyed no sooner but despisèd straight,°
Past reason hunted,[4] and no sooner had,
Past reason hated as a swallowed bait
On purpose laid to make the taker mad;   8
Mad in pursuit, and in possession so,[5]
excessive; intense   Had, having, and in quest to have, extreme;°
A bliss in proof, and proved, a very woe;[6]
Before, a joy proposed; behind, a dream.[7]   12
  All this the world well knows, yet none knows well
  To shun the heaven that leads men to this hell.[8]

1   *are nothing like the sun*

    Do not look like the sun at all
    (rejecting the traditional imagery
    of praise for female beauty familiar
    from Petrarchan love poetry)

2   *If hairs be wires*

    If hair is (traditionally compared to)
    finely spun gold wire

3   *belied with false compare*

    Misrepresented by exaggerated
    comparisons

130

My mistress' eyes are nothing like the sun;[1]
Coral is far more red than her lips' red;
If snow be white, why then her breasts are dun;° *grayish brown*
If hairs be wires,[2] black wires grow on her head. 4
I have seen roses damasked,° red and white, *spotted*
But no such roses see I in her cheeks;
And in some perfumes is there more delight
Than in the breath that from my mistress reeks.° *emanates* 8
I love to hear her speak, yet well I know
That music hath a far more pleasing sound.
I grant I never saw a goddess go;° *walk*
My mistress, when she walks, treads on the ground. 12
And yet, by Heaven, I think my love as rare° *precious*
As any she° belied with false compare.[3] *woman*

1   *Thou art as tyrannous, so as thou art, / As those whose beauties proudly make them cruel*

You are as pitiless, even as you are (i.e., dark), as those women conventionally regarded as beautiful are cruel.

2   *dear doting*

(1) Tenderly adoring; (2) painfully (expensively) devoted

3   *in good faith, some say, that thee behold*

In truth, some who see you say that

4   *the power to make love groan*

The ability to make lovers miserable

5   *to be sure that is not false*

To prove that my oath is not a lie

6   *swear / A thousand groans*

His *groans* replace the expected oaths that would be sworn to assert the truth of what is claimed.

7   *One on another's neck*

One right after the other

8   *Thy black is fairest in my judgment's place*

Your dark appearance is the most beautiful to my mind.

9   *save in thy deeds*

Except in your behavior (toward me)

10 *thence this slander, as I think, proceeds*

From this fact (of your cruel behavior toward me) the criticism of your beauty originates.

131

Thou art as tyrannous, so as thou art,
As those whose beauties proudly make them cruel,[1]
For well thou know'st to my dear doting[2] heart
Thou art the fairest and most precious jewel.   4
Yet, in good faith, some say, that thee behold,[3]
Thy face hath not the power to make love groan.[4]
To say they err I dare not be so bold,
Although I swear it to myself alone;   8
And to be sure that is not false,[5] I swear
merely A thousand groans[6] but° thinking on thy face;
One on another's neck[7] do witness bear
Thy black is fairest in my judgment's place.[8]   12
  In nothing art thou black save in thy deeds,[9]
  And thence this slander, as I think, proceeds.[10]

1   *Have put on black, and lovely mourners be*

    See Sonnet 127, lines 9 and 10.

2   *morning*

    **Unambiguously punning on
    "mourning."**

3   *becomes the gray cheeks of the east*

    Suits the gray half-light of the dawn

4   *that full star that ushers in the ev'n*

    I.e., Venus, the evening star

5   *sober*

    Somberly dressed; dark colored

6   *suit thy pity like in every part*

    **Let all your being (not just your
    eyes) show me pity.**

7   *all they foul that thy complexion lack*

    **That everyone is ugly who lacks
    your dark appearance**

132

Thine eyes I love, and they, as° pitying me, — *as if*
Knowing thy heart torment° me with disdain, — *torments*
Have put on black, and loving mourners be,[1]
Looking with pretty ruth° upon my pain; — *compassion*   4
And truly, not the morning[2] sun of heaven° — *i.e., the sky*
Better becomes the gray cheeks of the east,[3]
Nor that full° star that ushers in the ev'n[4] — *bright*
Doth half that glory to the sober[5] west   8
As those two mourning eyes become° thy face. — *suit*
Oh, let it then as well beseem° thy heart — *be appropriate to*
To mourn for me, since mourning doth thee grace,
And suit thy pity like in every part.[6]   12
  Then will I swear beauty herself is black,
  And all they foul that thy complexion lack.[7]

1   *But slave to slavery my sweet'st friend*
    must be

    **Without also making my dearest
    friend a complete slave**

2   *Me from myself thy cruel eye hath taken*

    **Your cruel eye has made me lose
    myself.**

3   *And my next self thou harder hast*
    engrossed

    **And you have even more cruelly
    taken control of my other self
    (i.e., my friend)**

4   *my friend's heart let my poor heart bail*

    **Let my unworthy heart serve as *bail*
    to release *my friend's heart*.**

5   *let my heart be his guard*

    **Permit my heart to be the jailor of
    his guardhouse**

6   *Thou canst not then use rigor in my jail*

    **I.e., in which case you cannot mis-
    treat my friend (who is) confined in
    my heart**

7   *Perforce am thine, and all that is in me*

    **I am necessarily yours, as is ev-
    erything in me (i.e., including my
    friend who is locked in my heart).**

133

Beshrew° that heart that makes my heart to groan — *i.e., Curse*
For that deep wound it gives my friend and me.
Is 't not enough to torture me alone,
But slave to slavery my sweet'st friend must be?[1]   4
Me from myself thy cruel eye hath taken,[2]
And my next self thou harder hast engrossed;[3]
Of him, myself, and thee I am forsaken,
A torment thrice threefold thus to be crossed.° — *thwarted*   8
Prison° my heart in thy steel bosom's ward,° — *Imprison / care*
But then my friend's heart let my poor heart bail.[4]
Whoe'er keeps° me, let my heart be his guard;[5] — *imprisons*
Thou canst not then use rigor in my jail.[6]   12
   And yet thou wilt, for I being pent° in thee, — *imprisoned*
   Perforce am thine, and all that is in me.[7]

1   *mortgaged to thy will*

    **Bound to (1) your wishes; (2) your
    sexual appetite**

2   *so that other mine / Thou wilt restore*

    **In order that you will restore my
    other self (i.e., my friend)**

3   *He learned but surety-like to write for
    me / Under that bond that him as fast
    doth bind.*

    **He was persuaded to act as my guar-
    antor for the bond (between you
    and me) under the terms of which
    he was bound to you as firmly as
    I was.**

4   *The statute of thy beauty thou wilt take*

    **You will demand everything to
    which your beauty entitles you.**

5   *put'st forth all to use*

    **(1) Lends everything out at interest;
    (2) commits everything to sexual
    activity**

6   *sue*

    **(1) Will bring a lawsuit against; (2)
    will pursue romantically**

7   *through my unkind abuse*

    **(1) Because of the wrongs you have
    done to me; (2) because of the
    wrongs I have committed (against
    my friend)**

8   *the whole*

    **The entire debt (and perhaps with
    bawdy pun on "hole")**

134

So now° I have confessed that he is thine,

now that

And° I myself am mortgaged to thy will,[1]

And that

Myself I'll forfeit, so that other mine

Thou wilt restore[2] to be my comfort still.

4

But° thou wilt not, nor he will not be free,

Nonetheless

For thou art covetous, and he is kind.

He learned but surety-like to write for me

Under that bond that him as fast doth bind.[3]

8

The statute of thy beauty thou wilt take,[4]

Thou usurer, that put'st forth all to use,[5]

And sue[6] a friend came° debtor for my sake;

who became a

So him I lose through my unkind abuse.[7]

12

  Him have I lost; thou hast both him and me;

  He pays the whole,[8] and yet am I not free.

1   *thy Will*

On the sonnet's play on the word "will" see LONGER NOTES on page 364. The capitalization of the word "will" in this sonnet and the next follow those of Q.

2   *to boot*

In addition; as well

3   *More than enough am I*

I (your William) am more than enough Will for you (i.e., you do not need additional lovers).

4   *that vex thee still*

That harass you constantly (with my sexual advances)

5   *To thy sweet will making addition thus*

I.e., by vexing you adding another will (mine) to yours

6   *large*

(1) Capacious; (2) lustful; excessive in desire; (3) generous

7   *once vouchsafe to hide my will in thine*

(1) Once and for all, see fit to join our wishes together; (2) just this one time allow me to put my sex organ in yours

8   *will in others*

Other men's desires

9   *fair acceptance*

Gracious welcome

10   *his store*

Its supply

11   *Let no unkind "no" fair beseechers kill*

Do not let an ungenerous refusal devastate any earnest suitor.

12   *Think all but one, and me in that one Will*

You should consider that all your suitors (*beseechers*) are really only one, and I am that one *Will* (in all of its senses).

135

Whoever° hath her wish, thou hast thy Will,[1]
And Will to boot,[2] and Will in overplus;°
More than enough am I[3] that vex thee still,[4]
To thy sweet will making addition thus.[5]   4

Wilt thou, whose will is large[6] and spacious,
Not once vouchsafe to hide my will in thine?[7]
Shall will in others[8] seem right gracious,°
And in my will no fair acceptance[9] shine?   8

The sea, all water, yet receives rain still,
And in abundance addeth to his store,[10]
So thou, being rich in Will, add to thy Will
One will of mine, to make thy large Will more.   12

Let no unkind "no" fair beseechers kill;[11]
Think all but one, and me in that one Will.[12]

Whatever woman — gloss for line 1 (Whoever)
excess — gloss for line 2 (overplus)
attractive — gloss for line 7 (gracious)

1   *come so near*

(1) Hit so close to home with my criticism; (2) come so close to (with sexual intent)

2   *blind soul*

Blind because the *soul* is unable to verify its intuitions with sense data

3   *I was thy Will*

(1) I was the man you desired; (2) I was your William. See LONGER NOTES on page 364.

4   *fulfill the treasure of thy love*

(1) Emotionally satisfy the precious thing that your love is; (2) fill full your vagina (c.f., *Hamlet* 1.3.30: "your chaste treasure open"); (3) fill up the treasure chest in which you keep what you love.

5   *my will one*

(1) My will one of these; (2) my will alone (with "will" in either case carrying multiple suggestions including, if not primarily here, "penis")

6   *In things of great receipt*

Inside of *things* with a great capacity (or *In* could mean "in terms of")

7   *Among a number one is reckoned none*

Among many, a single one goes unnoticed (playing on the proverb "one is no number").

8   *Though in thy store's account I one must be*

Although I must be inventoried as one of your abundant lovers (though also continuing the numerical joking that begins in line 6)

9   *For nothing hold me*

Consider me to be nothing

10   *That nothing me*

That inconsequential thing that I am

136

reproach	If thy soul check° thee that I come so near,[1]
	Swear to thy blind soul[2] that I was thy Will,[3]
	And will, thy soul knows, is admitted there;
charity	Thus far for love° my love-suit, sweet, fulfill.
	Will will fulfill the treasure of thy love,[4]
	Ay, fill it full with wills, and my will one.[5]
demonstrate	In things of great receipt[6] with ease we prove°
	Among a number one is reckoned none.[7]
multitude / uncounted	Then in the number° let me pass untold,°
	Though in thy store's account I one must be;[8]
	For nothing hold me,[9] so it please thee hold
	That nothing me,[10] a something sweet to thee.
only / always	Make but° my name thy love, and love that still,°
because	And then thou lov'st me, for° my name is Will.

4

8

12

1 *Love*

The poem is addressed to the personification of love as the blind, infant figure of Cupid.

2 *where it lies*

(1) Where beauty resides; (2) where it deceives

3 *what the best is, take the worst to be*

Regard as the best what is actually the worst

4 *corrupt by over-partial looks*

Distorted by looking with too much fondness

5 *Be anchored in the bay where all men ride*

I.e., are fixed upon that which all men desire. (*Ride* means in this context "move up and down on the tides" and thus lends itself to sexual suggestion.)

6 *Why of eyes' falsehood hast thou forgèd hooks, / Whereto the judgment of my heart is tied?*

Why have you out of my eye's delusion made hooks that snare my heart?

7 *a several plot*

An enclosed individually owned piece of property

8 *the wide world's common place*

A public area open to the entire world. (*Common* also could mean "promiscuous.")

9 *To put fair truth upon so foul a face*

In order to attribute virtuous qualities to such a corrupt sight

10 *things right true*

(1) Plainly visible truths; (2) faithful sex organs (*things*)

11 *And to this false plague are they now transferred*

And my heart and eyes are now given over to (1) this error of bad judgment; (2) this unfaithful woman

137

Thou blind fool, Love,[1] what dost thou to mine eyes
understand That they behold and see° not what they see?
They know what beauty is, see where it lies,[2]
Yet what the best is, take the worst to be.[3]   4
If eyes, corrupt by over-partial looks,[4]
Be anchored in the bay where all men ride,[5]
Why of eyes' falsehood hast thou forgèd hooks,
Whereto the judgment of my heart is tied?[6]   8
Why should my heart think that a several plot[7]
knows to be Which my heart knows° the wide world's common
place?[8]
Or why should / not so Or° mine eyes, seeing this, say this is not,°
To put fair truth upon so foul a face?[9]   12
In things right true[10] my heart and eyes have erred,
And to this false plague are they now transferred.[11]

1   *made of truth*

Completely honest (with a play on "maid *of truth*," i.e., a virgin)

2   *lies*

(1) Does not tell the truth; (2) goes to bed with other men

3   *false subtleties*

Deceptive ruses

4   *vainly*

(1) As a result of my vanity; (2) in vain, ineffectively

5   *Simply I credit*

Like a simpleton, or without difficulty, I believe (or tell myself that I believe)

6   *simple truth*

(1) Basic honesty; (2) obvious facts; (3) oversimplified reality

7   *says she not she is unjust*

Doesn't she say she is unfaithful (or dishonest)

8   *best habit*

(1) Finest clothing or adornment; (2) most useful pattern of behavior

9   *seeming trust*

(1) The feigning of mutual fidelity; (2) pretending to believe one another

10   *age in love loves not t' have years told*

An old person *in love* does not like to have his age disclosed.

11   *lie with*

(1) Tell lies along with; (2) have sex with

12   *in our faults*

(1) Engaged in our vices; (2) with regard to our weaknesses

13   *by lies we flattered be*

(1) We are made to feel better about ourselves by the lies we tell each other and ourselves; (2) by the lies we tell each other and ourselves we are deluded; (3) by laying together in having sex we are gratified. (Note also the shift from the singular pronouns in line 13 to the plural pronouns of line 14, enacting the mutuality the poem willingly endorses.)

138

mistress	When my love° swears that she is made of truth [1]
	I do believe her, though I know she lies, [2]
So that / inexperienced	That° she might think me some untutored° youth
Unskilled	Unlearnèd° in the world's false subtleties. [3] 4
	Thus vainly [4] thinking that she thinks me young,
	Although she knows my days are past the best,
	Simply I credit [5] her false-speaking tongue;
	On both sides thus is simple truth [6] suppressed. 8
why	But wherefore° says she not she is unjust? [7]
	And wherefore say not I that I am old?
	Oh, love's best habit [8] is in seeming trust, [9]
	And age in love loves not t' have years told. [10] 12
	Therefore I lie with [11] her, and she with me,
	And in our faults [12] by lies we flattered be. [13]

1 *call not me*

Do not ask me

2 *Wound me not with thine eye but with thy tongue*

I.e., Hurt me with the things you say (tell me you have other lovers), but not with your wandering eye (that gazes at other men).

3 *Use power with power, and slay me not by art*

Use the power you have over me directly, and do not hurt me with deceptive stratagems.

4 *thou lov'st elsewhere*

You have other lovers.

5 *but in my sight, / Dear heart, forbear to glance thine eye aside*

But when you are with me, my love, refrain from looking (at other men)

6 *need'st thou wound with cunning when thy might / Is more than my o'er-pressed defense can bide*

Do you need to hurt me with stratagems when your strength (i.e., the *art* and *power* in line 4) is too much for my overwhelmed defenses to withstand?

7 *my love*

My beloved

8 *turns my foes*

I.e., shifts her gaze

9 *Kill me outright with looks*

Just kill me now with your look (invoking the idea that a lover's glance might, like the mythological basilisk's, literally kill).

139

Oh, call not me[1] to justify the wrong
That thy unkindness lays upon my heart.
Wound me not with thine eye but with thy tongue;[2]
Use power with power, and slay me not by art.[3]   4
Tell me thou lov'st elsewhere;[4] but in my sight,
Dear heart, forbear to glance thine eye aside.[5]
Why   What° need'st thou wound with cunning when thy might
     Is more than my o'er-pressed defense can bide?[6]   8
Let me excuse thee: ah, my love[7] well knows
glances   Her pretty looks° have been mine enemies,
away from   And therefore from° my face she turns my foes,[8]
So that   That° they elsewhere might dart their injuries.   12
nearly   Yet do not so, but, since I am near° slain,
end   Kill me outright with looks[9] and rid° my pain.

1   *my pity-wanting pain*

My pain that lacks, or craves, pity

2   *better it were, / Though not to love, yet,*
     love, to tell me so

It would be better, even though you
don't love me, my love, nonetheless to tell me that you do.

3   *No news but health from their physicians*
     know

Hear only good news about their
health from their doctors

4   *this ill-wresting world*

This present age, which maliciously
interprets everything

5   *Bear thine eyes straight, though thy*
     proud heart go wide

Look steadily at me, even though
your desires wander elsewhere.
(The metaphor comes from
archery; the mistress' eyes are
likened to arrows, which may either
be aimed directly at the speaker, or
shot wide of the target, i.e., at other
lovers.)

140

Be wise° as thou art cruel; do not press°

My tongue-tied patience with too much disdain,

Lest sorrow lend me words, and words express

The manner of my pity-wanting pain.[1]   4

If I might teach thee wit,° better it were,

Though not to love, yet, love, to tell me so,[2]

As° testy° sick men, when their deaths be near,

No news but health from their physicians know.[3]   8

For if I should despair I should grow mad,

And in my madness might speak ill of thee.

Now this ill-wresting world[4] is grown so bad,

Mad slanderers by mad ears° believèd be.   12

That I may not be so,° nor thou belied,°

Bear thine eyes straight, though thy proud heart go

wide.[5]

as wise / oppress

intelligence; cleverness

Justs as / ill-tempered

i.e., listeners

i.e., slanderous / slandered

1 *Who in despite of view is pleased to dote*

My heart, regardless of what the
eyes may see, chooses to adore

2 *Nor tender feeling to base touches prone*

Nor is my sensitive sense of touch
susceptible to sexual stimulation

3 *Nor taste, nor smell*

Nor does my sense of taste, or smell

4 *from serving thee*

(1) From being your devoted
servant; (2) from providing a sexual
service to you

5 *leaves unswayed the likeness of a man*

Leaves ungoverned what is the
mere image of a man (since *my
heart* is serving elsewhere)

6 *vassal wretch*

Miserable, obedient servant

7 *Only my plague thus far I count my
gain*

To this degree I consider what
torments me to be an advantage

8 *awards me pain*

(1) Imposes my punishment now
(instead of my having to await
it in the afterlife); (2) makes me
miserable (which masochistically
I enjoy?)

141

In faith,° I do not love thee with mine eyes, *truth*
For they in thee a thousand errors° note, *defects*
But 'tis my heart that loves what they despise,
Who° in despite of view is pleased to dote.[1] *Which* 4
Nor° are mine ears with thy tongue's tune delighted, *Neither*
Nor tender feeling to base touches prone,[2]
Nor taste, nor smell,[3] desire to be invited
To any sensual feast with thee alone. 8
But° my five wits, nor my five senses, can *But neither*
Dissuade one foolish heart from serving thee,[4]
Who° leaves unswayed the likeness of a man,[5] *Which*
Thy proud heart's slave and vassal wretch[6] to be. 12
  Only my plague thus far I count my gain:[7]
  That she that° makes me sin awards me pain.[8] *who*

1   *Hate of my sin, grounded on sinful loving*

I.e., your hate for my sin (1) on
the grounds it is merely lust; (2)
determined by the fact that you are
lusting after others

2   *scarlet ornaments*

A religious metaphor: the redness
of her lips is like a cardinal's vest-
ment or the Whore of Babylon's
scarlet robe in Revelation 17:19

3   *sealed false bonds of love*

Confirmed (with kisses) false
promises of love

4   *Robbed others' beds' revenues of their
rents*

I.e., committed adultery with married men (the metaphor is of the
marital bed as an income-yielding
estate)

5   *Be it lawful*

May it be permissible that

6   *Whom thine eyes woo as mine importune
thee*

Who your eyes try to win as mine try
to win you

7   *Thy pity may deserve to pitied be*

(1) Your display of pity might make
you deserving of the same; (2) your
pitiable condition might deserve to
be pitied.

8   *to have what thou dost hide*

To have the pity that you withhold
from me

9   *By self-example mayst thou be denied*

May you be refused pity by your
own example.

142

Love is my sin, and thy dear° virtue hate, — *most precious*

Hate of my sin, grounded on sinful loving.[1]

Oh, but° with mine compare thou thine own state,° — *rely / (moral) condition*

And thou shalt find it° merits not reproving;° — *i.e., my state / criticism*   4

Or, if it do, not from those lips of thine

That have profaned their scarlet ornaments[2]

And sealed false bonds of love[3] as oft as mine,

Robbed others' beds' revenues of their rents.[4]   8

Be it lawful[5] I love thee as thou lov'st those

Whom thine eyes woo as mine importune thee.[6]

Root° pity in thy heart, that,° when it grows, — *Implant / so that*

Thy pity may deserve to pitied be.[7]   12

   If thou dost seek to have what thou dost hide,[8]

   By self-example mayst thou be denied.[9]

1   *feathered creatures*

    I.e., chickens

2   *holds her in chase*

    Runs after her

3   *bent / To follow*

    Focused on following

4   *flies*

    **I.e., flees; runs away (as in line 9,
    but here with a play on the literal
    sense as the chicken tries to fly
    away)**

5   *catch thy hope*

    **Catch up with (or, capture) what you
    are seeking**

6   *Will*

    **(1) William; (2) desire (the capitaliza-
    tion follows Q; see Sonnets 135
    and 136)**

143

Lo, as a careful° housewife runs to catch   *busy; attentive*
One of her feathered creatures[1] broke° away,   *that has run*
Sets down her babe, and makes all swift dispatch°   *haste*
In pursuit of the thing she would have stay,   4
Whilst her neglected child holds her in chase,[2]
Cries to catch her whose busy care is bent
To follow[3] that which flies[4] before her face,
Not prizing° her poor infant's discontent;   *paying attention to*   8
So° run'st thou after that which flies from thee,   *In exactly that way*
Whilst I, thy babe, chase thee afar behind.
But if thou catch thy hope,[5] turn back to me
And play the mother's part: kiss me; be kind.   12
  So will I pray that thou mayst have thy Will,[6]
  If thou turn back and my loud crying still.°   *pacify; silence*

1   *Two loves*

     (1) Two lovers; (2) two types of love

2   *spirits*

     Supernatural beings (i.e., angels
     or devils)

3   *suggest me still*

     Continually tempt me (toward good
     or evil)

4   *right fair*

     (1) Truly beautiful; (2) perfectly fair
     complexioned

5   *colored ill*

     Unpleasingly complexioned (i.e.,
     dark)

6   *hell*

     The slang sense "vagina" is present
     here and throughout the poem.

7   *my saint*

     I.e., my good angel

8   *foul pride*

     Overbearing lust

9   *whether that*

     Whether or not

10   *Suspect I may, yet not directly tell*

     I have reason to suspect, but I
     cannot tell with certainty

11   *But being both from me, both to each
     friend*

     But as they both are away from me
     and are friendly with one another

12   *I guess one angel in another's hell*

     I suspect that the evil angel has the
     good angel in her power (though
     hell in its slang sense strengthens
     the suggestion to make the poet
     suspect that his *Two loves* are
     sleeping together).

13   *shall I ne'er know*

     I will never know for a fact

14   *fire my good one out*

     I.e., drive my good angel away. *Fire*
     does not yet have the sense "to dis-
     miss from some position," rather it
     means here either "drive away with
     fire" (in which case *fire* refers per-
     haps to the woman's hot temper or
     conceivably the burning of venereal
     disease) or "expel" or "eject."

144

one of/and one Two loves[1] I have, of° comfort and° despair,
Which, like two spirits,[2] do suggest me still:[3]
The better angel is a man right fair,[4]
The worser spirit a woman colored ill.[5]   4
To win me soon to hell,[6] my female evil
Tempteth my better angel from my side,
And would corrupt my saint[7] to be a devil,
Wooing his purity with her foul pride.[8]   8
And whether that[9] my angel be turned fiend
Suspect I may, yet not directly tell,[10]
But being both from me, both to each friend,[11]
I guess one angel in another's hell.[12]   12
  Yet this shall I ne'er know,[13] but live in doubt,
  Till my bad angel fire my good one out.[14]

1   *Those lips that Love's own hand did make*

I.e., the woman's lips, which were fashioned by Love himself.

2   *for her sake*

Because of her (i.e., the woman who said *"I hate"*)

3   *Straight in*

Immediately into

4   *Was used in giving gentle doom*

Was normally employed in giving mild sentences

5   *thus anew to greet*

To address me thus:

6   *"I hate" from hate away she threw*

She removed the phrase *"I hate"* from the emotion the poet fears it expressed. *Hate away* possibly puns on the name of Shakespeare's wife Anne Hathaway. (This sonnet is the only one written in a tetrameter line.)

145

Those lips that Love's own hand did make [1]
Breathed forth the sound that said "I hate"
To me that languished for her sake; [2]
But when she saw my woeful state,   4
Straight in [3] her heart did mercy come,
Chiding that tongue that, ever sweet,
Was used in giving gentle doom, [4]
And taught it thus anew to greet: [5]   8
"I hate" she altered with an end
That followed it as gentle day
which Doth follow night, who° like a fiend
From Heaven to Hell is flown away.   12
  "I hate" from hate away she threw [6]
adding And saved my life, saying° "not you."

1   *Poor soul, the center of my sinful earth*

The speaker addresses his own soul, which is figured as the core of his corrupt body.

2   [   ]

See LONGER NOTE on page 365.

3   *these rebel powers that thee array*

(Subjected to) these uncontrollable forces (i.e., the body and its appetites) that enclose you

4   *pine within and suffer dearth*

Starve on the inside and tolerate deprivation

5   *Painting thy outward walls so costly gay*

Spending so much to adorn your body

6   *having so short a lease*

Since you inhabit (your body) for so short a time

7   *thy fading mansion*

I.e., your deteriorating body

8   *excess*

(1) Unneeded accumulation; (2) extravagance

9   *live thou upon thy servant's loss*

Sustain yourself by the body's inevitable decay

10   *let that pine to aggravate thy store*

Allow the body to waste away so that you may increase your store of riches.

11   *Buy terms divine in selling hours of dross*

Purchase time in Heaven by getting rid of hours wasted on worthless pleasure.

12   *that feeds on men*

That consumes all humankind

146

Poor soul, the center of my sinful earth,[1]
[   ][2] these rebel powers that thee array,[3]
Why dost thou pine within and suffer dearth,[4]
Painting thy outward walls so costly gay?[5]   4

expense Why so large cost,° having so short a lease,[6]
Dost thou upon thy fading mansion[7] spend?
Shall worms, inheritors of this excess,[8]
xpenditure/fate; purpose Eat up thy charge?° Is this thy body's end?°   8

Then, soul, live thou upon thy servant's loss,[9]
And let that pine to aggravate thy store;[10]
Buy terms divine in selling hours of dross;[11]
Internally/externally Within° be fed, without° be rich no more.   12

So shalt thou feed on death, that feeds on men,[12]
And death once dead, there's no more dying then.

1   *My love*

Refers here to the speaker's emotion rather than to his beloved (as
also in line 5)

2   *longer nurseth the disease*

Feeds the disease, allowing it to
live longer

3   *Th' uncertain sickly appetite to please*

To satisfy the capricious desire
brought on by sickness

4   *prescriptions are not kept*

Recommendations are not
followed

5   *I, desperate, now approve / Desire is*
    death, which physic did except

Despairing (or extremely ill) I understand now that desire, which my
physician did forbid, leads to death.

6   *Past cure I am, now reason is past care*

Now that reason ceases to care
about me (or, ceases to take care of
me), I am beyond any remedy.

7   *frantic mad*

Frenzied

8   *At random from the truth vainly*
    expressed

I.e., unable to perceive or articulate
the truth

147

My love[1] is as° a fever, longing still°   *like / always*
For that which longer nurseth the disease,[2]
Feeding on that which doth preserve the ill,°   *sickness*
Th' uncertain sickly appetite to please.[3]   4
My reason, the physician to my love,
Angry that his prescriptions are not kept,[4]
Hath left me, and I, desperate, now approve
Desire is death, which physic did except.[5]   8
Past cure I am, now reason is past care,[6]
And, frantic mad[7] with evermore° unrest,   *constant*
My thoughts and my discourse° as madmen's are,   *speech*
At random from the truth vainly expressed;[8]   12
  For I have sworn thee° fair and thought thee bright,   *that you are*
  Who art as black as Hell, as dark as night.

1   *Which have no correspondence with true sight*

    Which have no connection with actual vision

2   *Or, if they have, where is my judgment fled / That censures falsely what they see aright?*

    Or, if my eyes do see truly, where has my judgment gone, which misvalues what my eyes see correctly?

3   *If that be fair whereon my false eyes dote*

    If she is beautiful (or kind) on whom my unreliable eyes linger obsessively

4   *What means the world*

    What does it mean for everyone else

5   *If it be not, then love doth well denote / Love's eye is not so true as all men's*

    I.e., if my mistress really is not fair then my loving well demonstrates that the eyes of lovers see not as accurately as those of other people.

6   *vexed with watching and with tears*

    Troubled with sleepless nights and weeping

7   *No marvel then though I mistake my view*

    So it is no surprise that I misconstrue what I see

8   *thy foul faults should find*

    Discover your (1) physical flaws; or (2) immoral actions.

148

O me! What eyes hath love put in my head,
Which have no correspondence with true sight?[1]
Or, if they have, where is my judgment fled
That censures falsely what they see aright?[2]   4
If that be fair whereon my false eyes dote,[3]
What means the world[4] to say it is not so?
If it be not, then love doth well denote
Love's eye is not so true as all men's:[5] no,   8
How can it? Oh, how can love's eye be true,
That is so vexed with watching and with tears?[6]
No marvel then though I mistake my view;[7]
the sky   The sun itself sees not till heaven° clears.   12
clever; crafty   O cunning° love! With tears thou keep'st me blind,
     Lest eyes well-seeing thy foul faults should find.[8]

1   *When I against myself with thee partake*

When I take your side against myself

2   *when I forgot / Am of myself, all tyrant for thy sake*

When I ignore my own interests and become a tyrant to everyone on your behalf

3   *On whom*

I.e., is there anyone on whom

4   *if thou lour'st on me, do I not spend / Revenge upon myself with present moan*

If you scowl at me, do I not punish myself by immediately suffering?

5   *That is so proud thy service to despise*

That is so presumptuous that it would refuse to serve you

6   *all my best doth worship thy defect*

My best qualities adore your imperfection.

7   *love, hate on*

Continue hating me, my love

8   *thy mind*

What you are thinking

9   *Those that can see, thou lov'st, and I am blind*

You love only those who can see (to admire your beauty) and I am blind.

149

Canst thou, O cruel, say I love thee not,
When I against myself with thee partake?[1]
<small>about</small> Do I not think on° thee, when I forgot
Am of myself, all tyrant for thy sake?[2]   4

<small>Is there anyone who</small> Who° hateth thee that I do call my friend?
On whom[3] frown'st thou that I do fawn upon?
Nay, if thou lour'st on me, do I not spend
Revenge upon myself with present moan?[4]   8

<small>good quality</small> What merit° do I in myself respect
That is so proud thy service to despise,[5]
When all my best doth worship thy defect,[6]
<small>persuasion</small> Commanded by the motion° of thine eyes?   12

But, love, hate on,[7] for now I know thy mind:[8]
Those that can see, thou lov'st, and I am blind.[9]

1   *from what power hast thou*

From what supernatural power do you derive

2   *With insufficiency my heart to sway*

To rule my heart by means of imperfection (see Sonnet 149, line 11)

3   *give the lie to my true sight*

Call my accurate vision a liar

4   *that brightness doth not grace the day*

Assert that sunshine does not make the day more beautiful (i.e., make absurd declarations)

5   *Whence hast thou this becoming of things ill*

From where do you derive this power to beautify bad or ugly things?

6   *very refuse of thy deeds*

The foulest of your actions

7   *warrantise of skill*

Self-assurance

8   *thy worst all best exceeds*

Your worst actions seem better than everyone else's best.

9   *what others do abhor*

I.e., you, whom others find abhorrent

10 *With others thou shouldst not abhor my state*

You should not join with others in loathing my condition.

11 *If thy unworthiness raised love in me, / More worthy I to be beloved of thee.*

I.e., since there was so little to inspire me to love you, I am more deserving of your love in return.

150

Oh, from what power hast thou[1] this pow'rful might
With insufficiency my heart to sway,[2]
To make me give the lie to my true sight,[3]
And swear that brightness doth not grace the day?[4]   4
Whence hast thou this becoming of things ill,[5]
That in the very refuse of thy deeds[6]
There is such strength and warrantise of skill[7]
That in my mind thy worst all best exceeds?[8]   8
Who taught thee how to make me love thee more,
The more I hear and see just cause of hate?
Oh, though I love what others do abhor,[9]
With others thou shouldst not abhor my state.[10]   12
　If thy unworthiness raised love in me,
　More worthy I to be beloved of thee.[11]

1 *Love is too young*

(1) My love is too new; (2) Cupid is too young

2 *conscience*

Consciousness of right and wrong

3 *gentle cheater*

An oxymoron, with *gentle* ameliorating *cheater*, addressed to the unfaithful mistress

4 *urge not my amiss*

(1) Do not charge me with wrongdoing; (2) do not encourage me to behave badly.

5 *Lest guilty of my faults thy sweet self prove*

In case you turn out to be guilty of the same wrongs

6 *thou betraying me*

(1) Since you have been unfaithful to me; (2) since you have exposed my moral failings

7 *My nobler part*

I.e., my soul

8 *doth point out thee*

Turns its attention to you

9 *this pride*

(1) His conquest; (2) his erection

10 *To stand in thy affairs, fall by thy side*

(1) Like a soldier, to stand guard over your concerns, or die fighting for you; (2) to be erect in your vagina, and fall limp next to you

11 *No want of conscience hold it*

Do not consider it a lack of conscience (see note 2 above)

12 *for whose dear love*

(1) For the sake of the precious love of whom; (2) as a result of the precious love of whom; (3) to gain the precious love of whom

151

Love is too young[1] to know what conscience[2] is,
Yet who knows not conscience is born of love?
Then, gentle cheater,[3] urge not my amiss,[4]
Lest guilty of my faults thy sweet self prove;[5]   4
For, thou betraying me,[6] I do betray
My nobler part[7] to my gross body's treason.
has permission to   My soul doth tell my body that he may°
i.e., The penis / waits for   Triumph in love. Flesh° stays° no farther reason,   8
But, rising at thy name, doth point out thee[8]
As his triumphant prize; proud of this pride,[9]
servant   He is contented thy poor drudge° to be,
To stand in thy affairs, fall by thy side.[10]   12
   No want of conscience hold it[11] that I call
   Her "love" for whose dear love[12] I rise and fall.

1   *am forsworn*

  Have broken my oath

2   *twice forsworn to me love swearing*

  Doubly forsworn by swearing your love to me

3   *In act thy bed-vow broke, and new faith torn*

  I.e., in the act of having sex with me breaking your marital vows, and now have violated the pledge you made to me

4   *In vowing new hate after new love bearing*

  By now professing hate so soon after accepting love (with *bearing* carrying a sexual sense)

5   *misuse*

  Slander; misrepresent

6   *my honest faith in thee is lost*

  (1) My simple faith in you is gone; (2) my honesty is betrayed in the lies I tell about you.

7   *enlighten thee*

  Not the modern sense "make you wiser," but a literalizing claim: make you lighter (i.e., more beautiful)

8   *gave eyes to blindness*

  Chose to close my eyes; gave my eyes over *to blindness*

9   *swear against*

  Give perjured evidence contrary to

10 *eye*

  With a pun on "I"

11 *To swear against the truth so foul a lie*

  To swear to a vile *lie* that is so contrary to the *truth*

152

In loving thee thou know'st I am forsworn,[1]
But thou art twice forsworn to me love swearing,[2]
In act thy bed-vow broke, and new faith torn[3]
In vowing new hate after new love bearing.[4]   4
But why of two oaths' breach do I accuse thee
When I break twenty? I am perjured most,
designed only For all my vows are oaths but° to misuse[5] thee,
And all my honest faith in thee is lost;[6]   8
For I have sworn deep oaths of thy deep kindness,
Oaths of thy love, thy truth, thy constancy,
And, to enlighten thee,[7] gave eyes to blindness,[8]
Or made them swear against[9] the thing they see.   12
that you are For I have sworn thee° fair: more perjured eye,[10]
To swear against the truth so foul a lie.[11]

1 *laid by his brand*

Put down his torch (one of Cupid's common attributes)

2 *A maid of Dian's this advantage found*

A virginal nymph attending on Diana, the goddess of chastity, took advantage of this opportunity.

3 *of that ground*

Nearby

4 *of Love*

Belonging to Cupid

5 *a seething bath*

"Sweating tubs" were used to treat ailments, including venereal disease.

6 *A dateless lively heat, still to endure*

An endless vital heat, lasting forever (the fire of Cupid's torch has converted a cool pool of water into a hot spring, a classical myth widely circulating in the Renaissance)

7 *yet men prove / Against strange maladies a sovereign cure*

Men still find to be the best remedy for unusual diseases

8 *Love's brand new fired*

Cupid's torch having been relit

9 *for trial needs would*

To test it he would have to

10 *eye*

Q has *eye* (and it picks up the phrase of line 9), but some editors emend to "eyes" to make the couplet's rhyme exact.

153

Cupid laid by his brand [1] and fell asleep.
A maid of Dian's this advantage found, [2]
And his love-kindling fire did quickly steep
In a cold valley-fountain of that ground, [3]
Which borrowed from this holy fire of Love [4]
A dateless lively heat, still to endure, [5]
And grew° a seething bath, [6] which yet men prove
Against strange maladies a sovereign cure. [7]
But at° my mistress' eye Love's brand new fired, [8]
The boy° for trial needs would [9] touch my breast.
I, sick withal,° the help of bath desired,
And thither hied,° a sad distempered° guest,
But found no cure; the bath for my help lies
Where Cupid got new fire: my mistress' eye. [10]

became
with the flame from
i.e., Cupid
from it
hurried / diseased

4

8

12

1   *little love-god*

    Cupid

2   *fairest votary*

    **The most beautiful worshipper (of
Diana, goddess of chastity)**

3   *many legions*

    Great numbers

4   *the general of hot desire*

    I.e., Cupid, the ruler of passion

5   *in a cool well by*

    In a nearby pool of cold water

6   *took heat perpetual*

    Was heated eternally

7   *this by that I prove*

    **That experience demonstrates that
the following is true**

8   *Love's fire heats water; water cools not
love*

    **(1) Cupid's torch can heat up water,
but water cannot extinguish passion. (There is an ironic echo here
of the biblical Song of Solomon:
"Much water cannot quench love,
neither can the floods drown it"
(8:7).)**

154

The little love-god [1] lying once° asleep
i.e., one day

Laid° by his side his heart-inflaming brand,°
Had laid / torch

Whilst many nymphs that vowed chaste life to keep

Came tripping by; but in her maiden hand   4

The fairest votary [2] took up that fire,

Which many legions [3] of true hearts had warmed,

And so the general of hot desire [4]

Was, sleeping, by a virgin hand disarmed.   8

This brand she quenchèd in a cool well by, [5]

Which from love's fire took heat perpetual, [6]

Growing° a bath and healthful remedy
Becoming

For men diseased; but I, my mistress' thrall,°   12
slave

Came there for cure, and this by that I prove: [7]

Love's fire heats water; water cools not love. [8]

1   *A Lover's Complaint*

See Longer Note on page 366.

2   *concave womb reworded*

Hollowed-out side, or cave, echoed. (The sound of the echoed story is imagined to be born out of the hillside's womb.)

3   *plaintful story*

Mournful lament

4   *sist'ring vale*

Neighboring valley

5   *t' attend this double voice accorded*

Agreed to listen to this echoed voice (also see Longer Note on page 366).

6   *Storming her world with sorrow's wind and rain*

Ravaging her body with the sighs and tears of sadness

7   *plaited hive of straw*

Straw hat

8   *fortified her visage*

Shielded her face

9   *Whereon the thought might think sometime it saw / The carcass of a beauty spent and done*

A mind might suspect that it saw there the remnants of her beauty which has now faded away.

10 *scythèd all that youth begun*

Cut down all the beauty begun in youth

11 *fell rage*

Cruel fury

12 *peeped through lattice of seared age*

Was visible through the wrinkles of withered age

13 *heave her napkin to her eyne*

Raise her handkerchief to her eyes

14 *conceited characters*

Artfully arranged letters

15 *Laund'ring the silken figures in the brine*

Washing the embroidered words in her tears

16 *That seasoned woe had pelleted in tears*

That long-practiced sorrow had formed into pellet-like tears

17 *what contents it bears*

I.e., the words on her napkin, which presumably remind her of her former lover

18 *undistinguished*

Indistinguishable, unintelligible

19 *high and low*

(1) Loud and soft; (2) pitched in high and low tones

20 *levelled eyes their carriage ride, / As they did batt'ry to the spheres intend*

Eyeballs (here likened to cannon-balls) move and are focused as if they would assault the heavens

21 *poor balls are tied / To th' orbèd Earth*

Eyeballs are fixed on the spherical Earth

22 *right on*

Straight head

A Lover's Complaint [1]

From off a hill whose concave womb reworded [2]
A plaintful story [3] from a sist'ring vale, [4]
My spirits t' attend this double voice accorded, [5]
And down I laid to list° the sad-tuned tale;   *overhear; listen to*
Ere long espied a fickle° maid full° pale,   *anxious / completely*   5
Tearing of papers, breaking rings a-twain,°   *in half*
Storming her world with sorrow's wind and rain. [6]

Upon her head a plaited hive of straw, [7]
Which fortified her visage [8] from the sun,
Whereon the thought might think sometime it saw   10
The carcass of a beauty spent and done. [9]
Time had not scythèd all that youth begun, [10]
Nor youth all quit, but, spite of Heaven's fell rage, [11]
Some beauty peeped through lattice of seared age. [12]

Oft did she heave her napkin to her eyne, [13]   15
Which° on it had conceited characters, [14]   *I.e., the napkin*
Laund'ring the silken figures in the brine [15]
That seasoned woe had pelleted in tears, [16]
And often reading what contents it bears; [17]
As often shrieking undistinguished [18] woe,   20
In clamors° of all size, both high and low. [19]   *cries*

Sometimes her levelled eyes their carriage ride,
As they did batt'ry to the spheres intend; [20]
Sometime, diverted, their poor balls are tied
To th' orbèd Earth; [21] sometimes they do extend   25
Their view right on; [22] anon° their gazes lend   *next*
To every place at once and nowhere fixed,
The mind and sight distractedly commixed.°   *commingled*

1   *Proclaimed in her a careless hand of pride*
    Showed her to be free of pride

2   *descended her*
    Fell from her

3   *favors from a maund*
    Tokens of love out of a basket

4   *beaded jet*
    Black beads

5   *Like usury, applying wet to wet*
    **As lending with interest adds
    money to money, her tears add
    water to the river**

6   *monarch's hands that let not bounty fall
    / Where want cries "some," but where
    excess begs all*
    **Like kings who do not bestow riches
    upon those in need, but only upon
    those petitioners who are already
    wealthy**

7   *schedules*
    Pieces of paper

8   *posied*
    Inscribed with loving words

9   *With sleided silk feat and affectedly /
    Enswathed and sealed to curious secrecy*
    **With woven silk, neatly and lovingly
    wrapped, and sealed to keep them
    secret (to prevent others from see-
    ing them)**

10 *Ink would have seemed more black and
    damnèd here!'*
    **Ink would have been more truly
    menacing (than blood) for the writ-
    ing of these letters.**

11 *Big discontent so breaking*
    Her terrible anger thus destroying

neither / braid	Her hair, nor° loose nor tied in formal plait,°
	Proclaimed in her a careless hand of pride;[1] 30
straw	For some, untucked, descended her[2] sheaved° hat,
	Hanging her pale and pinèd cheek beside;
ribbon / remain	Some in her threaden fillet° still did bide,°
	And true to bondage would not break from thence,
loosely; carelessly	Though slackly° braided in loose negligence. 35

	A thousand favors from a maund[3] she drew
	Of amber, crystal, and of beaded jet,[4]
	Which one by one she in a river threw,
edge	Upon whose weeping margin° she was set,
	Like usury, applying wet to wet,[5] 40
	Or monarch's hands that lets not bounty fall
	Where want cries "some," but where excess begs all.[6]

	Of folded schedules[7] had she many a one,
threw in	Which she perused, sighed, tore, and gave° the flood;
	Cracked many a ring of posied[8] gold and bone 45
tombs	Bidding them find their sepulchers° in mud;
	Found yet more letters sadly penned in blood,
	With sleided silk feat and affectedly
	Enswathed and sealed to curious secrecy.[9]

flowing	These often bathed she in her fluxive° eyes, 50
	And often kissed, and often gave to tear,
record	Cried "O false blood, thou register° of lies,
untested; unreliable	What unapprovèd° witness dost thou bear!
	Ink would have seemed more black and damnèd
	here!"[10]
rips apart	This said, in top of rage the lines she rents,° 55
	Big discontent so breaking[11] their contents.

1   *a blusterer, that the ruffle knew*

   A braggart, with the ostentation

2   *The swiftest hours, observèd as they flew*

   **The rapidly passing days of youth,
but learned from them as they
passed**

3   *Towards this afflicted fancy fastly drew*

   **Rapidly approached this vision of
unhappiness**

4   *So slides he down upon his grainèd bat*

   **So he descends to the river's edge
leaning on his walking stick.**

5   *comely distant*

   At a respectable distance

6   *being sat*

   Having sat down

7   *If that from him there may be aught
applied / Which may her suffering ecstasy
assuage*

   **If he could offer any help to ease
her fit of sorrow**

8   *"Father"*

   **A term of respect for any older man.
See LONGER NOTE on page 366.**

9   *if I had self-applied / Love to myself and to
no love beside*

   **If I had loved myself and no one else
(as the young man is criticized for
doing in Sonnets 1–17)**

10   *I attended / A youthful suit*

   **I allowed myself to be courted by a
young man.**

11   *one by nature's outwards so commended /
That maidens' eyes stuck over all his face*

   **One whose appearance was so
blessed by nature that young
women could not take their eyes
off his face**

12   *Love lacked a dwelling*

   **Venus, goddess of love, had no
home.**

dignified / nearby A reverend° man that grazed his cattle nigh,°
Formerly Sometime° a blusterer, that the ruffle knew[1]
Of court, of city, and had let go by
The swiftest hours, observèd as they flew,[2]   60
Towards this afflicted fancy fastly drew,[3]
And, privileged by age, desires to know
In brief the grounds and motives of her woe.

So slides he down upon his grainèd bat,[4]
And comely distant[5] sits he by her side,   65
asks When he again desires° her, being sat,[6]
sorrow / share Her grievance° with his hearing to divide.°
If that from him there may be aught applied
Which may her suffering ecstasy assuage,[7]
'Tis promised in the charity of age.   70

"Father,"[8] she says, "though in me you behold
blighting; disgraceful The injury of many a blasting° hour,
Let it not tell your judgment I am old:
Not age, but sorrow over me hath power.
growing I might as yet have been a spreading° flower,   75
Fresh to myself, if I had self-applied
Love to myself and to no love beside.[9]

"But, woe is me! Too early I attended
A youthful suit[10]—it was to gain my grace;
Oh, one by nature's outwards so commended   80
That maidens' eyes stuck over all his face.[11]
Love lacked a dwelling,[12] and made him her place,
And when in his fair parts she did abide
She was new lodged and newly deified.

1 *every light occasion of the wind / Upon*
his lips their silken parcels hurls

With each small gust of wind, his
silky curls are tossed against his
lips.

2 *What's sweet to do, to do will aptly find*

That which is pleasant to do will get
done easily.

3 *on his visage was in little drawn / What*
largeness thinks in paradise was sawn

(The beauty) on his face was a min-
iature version of the great beauty
one imagines was cut in paradise.

4 *Small show of man*

Very little beard

5 *phoenix*

Glorious or rare, like the mythical
bird

6 *Whose bare out-bragged the web it seem'd*
to wear; / Yet showed his visage by that
cost more dear

The bareness of his chin outdid the
soft down it seemed to wear, yet
proved the excellence of his face
in that precious clothing (i.e., the
beard) it wore.

7 *nice affections wavering stood in doubt /*
If best were as it was, or best without

Scrupulous judges of taste wavered,
wondering if he was more attractive
with or without facial hair.

8 *maiden-tongued*

Soft, or gentle, in speech

9 *His rudeness so with his authorized*
youth / Did livery falseness in a pride of
truth.

His lack of refinement, acceptable
in someone who is young, clothed
dishonesty in the uniform of truth.

10 *That horse his mettle from his rider takes*

That his horse takes strength from
its rider

11 *noble by the sway*

Ennobled by being under his
control

12 *What rounds, what bounds, what course,*
what stop

What extraordinary control of the
horse he has (*rounds*, *bounds*, *course*,
and *stops* are all movements of a
well-trained horse)

13 *controversy hence a question takes: /*
Whether the horse by him became his
deed, / Or he his manage by th' well-doing
steed

This produces the question: does
the horse achieve his grace from
the rider's skill, or does the rider
derive his control from the talented
horse?

brownish "His browny° locks did hang in crooked curls,   85
And every light occasion of the wind
Upon his lips their silken parcels hurls.[1]
What's sweet to do, to do will aptly find:[2]
Each eye that saw him did enchant the mind,
For on his visage was in little drawn   90
What largeness thinks in paradise was sawn.[3]

"Small show of man[4] was yet upon his chin;
His phoenix[5] down began but to appear
indescribable Like unshorn velvet on that termless° skin,
Whose bare out-bragged the web it seemed to wear;   95
Yet showed his visage by that cost more dear,[6]
And nice affections wavering stood in doubt
If best were as it was, or best without.[7]

virtues "His qualities° were beauteous as his form,
forthcoming; frank For maiden-tongued[8] he was, and thereof free;°   100
provoked Yet, if men moved° him, was he such a storm
As oft 'twixt May and April is to see,
When winds breathe sweet, unruly though they be.
His rudeness so with his authorized youth
Did livery falseness in a pride of truth.[9]   105

"Well could he ride, and often men would say
That horse his mettle from his rider takes:[10]
i.e., its obedience Proud of subjection,° noble by the sway,[11]
What rounds, what bounds, what course, what stop[12]
        he makes!
And controversy hence a question takes: 110
Whether the horse by him became his deed,
Or he his manage by th' well-doing steed.[13]

1 *on this side*

I.e., on the former side (holding that the rider is responsible for the excellence)

2 *His real habitude gave life and grace / To appertainings*

His noble character enlivened and dignified everything he touched.

3 *not in his case*

Not merely in appearance

4 *made fairer by their place*

Made more beautiful by being attached to him

5 *yet their purposed trim / Pieced not his grace*

Yet their intended decoration did not add to his grace at all.

6 *replication prompt*

Quick response

7 *For his advantage still did wake and sleep*

I.e., arranged their schedules to serve his needs

8 *had the dialect and different skill*

Could speak in various linguistic and stylistic registers

9 *Catching all passions in his craft of will*

Controlling everyone's emotions with his rhetorical ability

10 *That he did in the general bosom reign*

So that he ruled in the hearts of everyone

11 *In personal duty, following where he haunted*

Devoted to his person, following him to the places he frequented

12 *Consents bewitched, ere he desire, have granted*

Bewitched by him, people grant their consent before he even asks for something.

13 *And dialogued for him what he would say*

And speak on his behalf

14 *in it put their mind*

They became obsessed with it.

15 *that in th' imagination set / The goodly objects which abroad they find / Of lands and mansions, theirs in thought assigned*

Who imagine that the impressive things, like *land and mansions*, that they see in the world, actually belong to them

16 *Than the true gouty landlord which doth owe them*

Than the gout-ridden owner who actually owns them

"But quickly on this side[1] the verdict went:
His real habitude gave life and grace
To appertainings[2] and to ornament,   115
Accomplished in himself, not in his case;[3]

adornments All aids,° themselves made fairer by their place,[4]
intending to be Came for° additions; yet their purposed trim
Pieced not his grace,[5] but were all graced by him.

persuasive "So on the tip of his subduing° tongue   120
All kind of arguments and question deep,
All replication prompt,[6] and reason strong,
For his advantage still did wake and sleep.[7]
To make the weeper laugh, the laugher weep,
He had the dialect and different skill,[8]   125
Catching all passions in his craft of will,[9]

"That he did in the general bosom reign[10]
Of young, of old, and sexes both enchanted,
To dwell with him in thoughts, or to remain
In personal duty, following where he haunted.[11]   130
Consents bewitched, ere he desire, have granted,[12]
And dialogued for him what he would say,[13]
Asked their own wills, and made their wills obey.

"Many there were that did his picture get
To serve their eyes, and in it put their mind,[14]   135
Like fools that in th' imagination set
The goodly objects which abroad they find
Of lands and mansions, theirs in thought assigned,[15]
And laboring in more pleasures to bestow them
Than the true gouty landlord which doth owe them.[16]   140

1   *was my own fee-simple*

All my own (a legal term for owner-
ship without limitation)

2   *Reserved the stalk and gave him all my*
    flower

Gave him what was most valuable
and kept for me what was worthless
(with a sense of being "deflow-
ered")

3   *as some my equals did, / Demand of him,*
    nor being desirèd yielded

As some other young maids did, ask
him for sexual favors, or consent
when he desired me

4   *With safest distance*

By keeping him at a distance

5   *Of proofs new-bleeding*

Out of this fresh evidence (of the injuries he has caused). *New-bleeding*
suggests their loss of virginity.

6   *which remained the foil / Of this false*
    jewel

I.e., his reputation makes him even
more appealing. (A *foil* is here the
background used to make a *jewel*
shine brighter)

7   *shunned by precedent*

Avoided on the basis of the experience of others

8   *Or forced examples, 'gainst her own*
    content, / To put the by-past perils in her
    way?

Or allowed historical examples to
dissuade her from what she wants
to do on the basis of those bygone
dangers

9   *Counsel may stop awhile what will not*
    stay

Wise advice will only temporarily
delay what someone does not want
to stop doing.

10 *when we rage, advice is often seen, /*
    By blunting us, to make our wits more
    keen

When we irrationally desire something, advice often, by inhibiting
us, makes us desire it more.

11 *stand aloof*

Stay away

12 *The one a palate hath that needs will taste*

I.e., appetite cannot help itself
from trying to satisfy its desires.

"So many have, that never touched his hand,
Sweetly supposed them mistress of his heart.
My woeful self, that did in freedom stand
And was my own fee-simple,[1] not in part,
What with his art in youth, and youth in art,   145
Threw my affections in his charmèd power,
Reserved the stalk and gave him all my flower.[2]

"Yet did I not, as some my equals did,
Demand of him, nor being desirèd yielded;[3]
Finding myself in honor so forbid,   150
With safest distance[4] I mine honor shielded.
Their experience Experience° for me many bulwarks builded
Of proofs new-bleeding,[5] which remained the foil
Of this false jewel,[6] and his amorous spoil.

"But, ah, who ever shunned by precedent[7]   155
experience; try out The destined ill she must herself assay?°
Or forced examples, 'gainst her own content,
To put the by-past perils in her way?[8]
Counsel may stop awhile what will not stay,[9]
For when we rage, advice is often seen,   160
By blunting us, to make our wits more keen.[10]

passion "Nor gives it satisfaction to our blood°
example That we must curb it upon others' proof,°
forbidden To be forbod° the sweets that seem so good
behalf For fear of harms that preach in our behoof.°   165
O appetite, from judgment stand aloof![11]
The one a palate hath that needs will taste,[12]
Though reason weep, and cry, 'It is thy last.'

1   *For further I could say*

    I could find more ways to say

2   *Heard where his plants in others'*
    orchards grew

    **I.e., heard about married women
    whom he impregnated**

3   *Knew vows were ever brokers to defiling*

    **Knew that his promises were only
    means to enable his seduction of
    young women**

4   *characters and words merely but art*

    **Written and spoken words de-
    signed only for deceit**

5   *held my city*

    **Protected my virginity (which was
    often imagined as a city or castle
    that needed defending from male
    invasion)**

6   *That's to ye sworn to none was ever said*

    **What I swear to you, I have never
    said to anyone.**

7   *For feasts of love I have been called unto, /
    Till now did ne'er invite*

    **I.e., I have been seduced before,
    but until now never was the
    seducer.**

8   *All my offences that abroad you see / Are
    errors of the blood*

    **All the transgressions that you see
    me commit in public are sins of
    passion.**

9   *with acture they may be*

    They may be committed

10 *They sought their shame that so their
    shame did find*

    **Those women I dishonored *sought
    their shame* (were asking for it).**

11 *so much less of shame in me
    remains / By how much of me their
    reproach contains*

    **I feel even less shame the more they
    reproach me (because of how much
    they are guilty of what they criticize
    me for).**

12 *Not one whose flame my heart so much as
    warmed*

    **There was not a single one who
    interested me at all**

13 *Kept hearts in liveries, but mine own was
    free*

    **Their hearts were like servants to
    me, but mine was free.**

unfaithful   "For further I could say[1] 'This man's untrue,'°
instances   And knew the patterns° of his foul beguiling,   170
                Heard where his plants in others' orchards grew,[2]
                Saw how deceits were gilded in his smiling,
                Knew vows were ever brokers to defiling,
                Thought characters and words merely but art,[4]
                And bastards of his foul adulterate heart.   175

                "And long upon these terms I held my city,[5]
began to   Till thus he 'gan° besiege me: 'Gentle maid,
                Have of my suffering youth some feeling pity,
                And be not of my holy vows afraid.
                That's to ye sworn to none was ever said,[6]   180
                For feasts of love I have been called unto,
                Till now did ne'er invite[7] nor never woo.

                " 'All my offences that abroad you see
                Are errors of the blood,[8] none of the mind;
                Love made them not: with acture they may be,[9]   185
neither   Where neither party is nor° true nor kind.
                They sought their shame that so their shame did find,[10]
                And so much less of shame in me remains
                By how much of me their reproach contains.[11]

                " 'Among the many that mine eyes have seen,   190
                Not one whose flame my heart so much as warmed,[12]
injury   Or my affection put to th' smallest teen,°
leisure hours Or any of my leisures° ever charmed:
                Harm have I done to them, but ne'er was harmed,
                Kept hearts in liveries, but mine own was free,[13]   195
                And reigned, commanding in his monarchy.

1   *wounded fancies*
    Heartbroken lovers

2   *aptly understood*
    Fittingly represented

3   *Encamped in hearts, but fighting out-
    wardly*

    **I.e., existing in the women's hearts,
    who are only pretending to resist
    me**

4   *With twisted metal amorously
    impleached*

    Intertwined with precious metals

5   *many a several fair*
    Many different beauties

6   *Their kind acceptance weepingly
    beseeched*

    **Desperately asking me to accept
    their entreaties**

7   *deep-brained sonnets*
    See LONGER NOTE on page 366.

8   *Whereto his invised properties did tend*

    **I.e., The diamond's properties sug-
    gest the young man's qualities of
    beauty and hardness (*invised* prob-
    ably means "unseen" but could be
    an error for "envied")**

9   *in whose fresh regard / Weak sights their
    sickly radiance do amend*

    **Which, in being looked at, can
    improve poor vision. (The emerald
    was sometimes thought to have the
    power to improve or even restore
    sight.)**

10 *The Heaven-hued sapphire and the opal
    blend / With objects manifold*

    **The blue sapphire and the opal
    combine to evoke a variety of the
    young man's qualities.**

11 *With wit well blazoned, smiled or made
    some moan*

    **Vividly described, seemed to smile
    or complain**

12 *Of pensived and subdued desires the
    tender*

    **The offering (*tender*) of sad and
    sober desire (in contrast to the
    trophies of affections hot)**

13 *where I myself must render*
    I.e., to whom I have to give them

14 *my origin and ender*
    The source of my life and death

15 *must your oblations be, / Since I their
    altar, you enpatron me*

    **Should by right be offered to you,
    since I am merely the altar at which
    they are left, while you are the
    patron saint for whom they are
    intended**

" 'Look here, what tributes wounded fancies[1] sent me,
Of pallid pearls and rubies red as blood,

Signifying Figuring° that they their passions likewise lent me
Of grief and blushes, aptly understood[2]   200
In bloodless white and the encrimsoned mood:

Signs Effects° of terror and dear modesty
Encamped in hearts, but fighting outwardly.[3]

treasures " 'And, lo, behold these talents° of their hair,
With twisted metal amorously impleached,[4]   205
I have received from many a several fair,[5]
Their kind acceptance weepingly beseeched,[6]

additions With the annexions° of fair gems enriched,
And deep-brained sonnets[7] that did amplify
Each stone's dear nature, worth, and quality.   210

" 'The diamond? Why, 'twas beautiful and hard,
Whereto his invised properties did tend;[8]
The deep-green emerald, in whose fresh regard
Weak sights their sickly radiance do amend;[9]
The Heaven-hued sapphire and the opal blend   215

different With objects manifold:[10] each several° stone,
With wit well blazoned, smiled or made some moan.[11]

" 'Lo, all these trophies of affections hot,
Of pensived and subdued desires the tender,[12]
Nature hath charged me that I hoard them not,   220
But yield them up where I myself must render[13]—
That is, to you, my origin and ender[14]—

necessity For these, of force,° must your oblations be,
Since I their altar, you enpatron me.[15]

1 *Whose white weighs down the airy scale of praise*

The whiteness of your hand out-weighs all praise that by compari-son can only be as light as air.

2 *Take all these similes to your own com-mand*

Apply to yourself all the flattering comparisons my former mistresses used to describe me.

3 *What me, your minister, for you obeys*

Whoever obeys me, the priest devoted to you, also obeys you.

4 *to your audit comes / Their distract parcels in combinèd sums*

I.e., the various gifts (given me) are now combined and placed in your account.

5 *device*

Emblematic token

6 *sister sanctified, of holiest note*

(If not a nun), one notable for her holiness

7 *Which late her noble suit in court did shun*

Who recently rejected the wooing of noble courtiers

8 *rarest havings*

Exceptional qualities

9 *spirits of richest coat*

Gentlemen of the noblest families

10 *thence remove / To spend her living in eternal love*

Left there to dedicate her life to the love of God

11 *what labor is't to leave / The thing we have not, mast'ring what not strives*

How hard could it be to give up something we do not have in the first place (referring to the nun, who shuns her earthly suitors), overcoming that which makes no resistance?

12 *Planing the place which did no form receive*

Smoothing the place on which no impression has been made

13 *Playing patient sports in unconstrainèd gyves*

Playing at patience in self-imposed shackles (which therefore can be taken off)

14 *that her fame so to herself contrives*

Whose reputation in this way invents for itself

15 *makes her absence valiant, not her might*

I.e., she keeps her chastity by fleeing temptation rather than withstanding it.

indescribable   " 'Oh, then, advance of yours that phraseless° hand,   225
Whose white weighs down the airy scale of
     praise;[1]
Take all these similes to your own command,[2]

Sanctified   Hallowed° with sighs that burning lungs did raise;
What me, your minister, for you obeys,[3]
Works under you, and to your audit comes   230
Their distract parcels in combinèd sums.[4]

" 'Lo, this device[5] was sent me from a nun,
Or sister sanctified, of holiest note,[6]
Which late her noble suit in court did shun,[7]

i.e., young courtiers   Whose rarest havings[8] made the blossoms°
     dote;   235
For she was sought by spirits of richest coat,[9]

she kept   But kept° cold distance, and did thence remove
To spend her living in eternal love.[10]

" 'But, oh, my sweet, what labor is't to leave
The thing we have not, mast'ring what not
     strives,[11]   240
Planing the place which did no form receive,[12]
Playing patient sports in unconstrainèd gyves?[13]
She that her fame so to herself contrives[14]
The scars of battle 'scapeth by the flight,
And makes her absence valiant, not her might.[15]   245

1   *Upon the moment did her force subdue*

Instantly brought her under my power

2   *And now she would the cagèd cloister fly*

And immediately she wanted to leave the convent

3   *Religious love put out religion's eye*

I.e., her passionate love (for me) ended her religious devotion.

4   *Not to be tempted would she be immured, / And now, to tempt, all liberty procured.*

To avoid temptation she had wanted to be closed up in the convent, and now to be tempted (or to tempt me) she obtained total freedom.

5   *Have emptied all their fountains in my well*

Have given up all their bounty to me

6   *mine I pour your ocean all among*

Now that this is mine I add it to your greater bounty.

7   *to physic your cold breast*

To cure your unresponsive heart

8   *Who, disciplined, ay, dieted in grace*

I.e., who had been subject to the discipline of the convent. (*Ay, dieted*, i.e., even dieted, intensifies the sense of the discipline she accepted.)

9   *t' assail begun*

Began to assault her (with my image)

10   *giving place*

Giving way; failing to hold their ground

11   *Vow, bond, nor space, / In thee hath neither sting, knot, nor confine*

In your domain, oaths, legal bonds, or physical confines have no power to hurt, bind, or restrict.

12   *impressest*

I.e., forcibly recruit to military service

13   *impediments*

Obstacles (to love)

14   *filial fear*

A daughter's fear of her father's anger

15   *Love's arms are peace*

Love's weapons enforce peace (since it overcomes everything).

16   *And sweetens, in the suff'ring pangs it bears*

(Love) assuages, in the acute suffering it is able to endure.

" 'Oh, pardon me, in that my boast is true:
good fortune   The accident° which brought me to her eye
Upon the moment did her force subdue,[1]
And now she would the cagèd cloister fly.[2]
Religious love put out religion's eye.[3]   250
Not to be tempted would she be immured,
And now, to tempt, all liberty procured.[4]

" 'How mighty then you are, oh, hear me tell!
hearts   The broken bosoms° that to me belong
Have emptied all their fountains in my well,[5]   255
And mine I pour your ocean all among.[6]
was strong   I strong° o'er them, and you o'er me being strong,
bring together   Must for your victory us all congest,°
As compound love to physic your cold breast.[7]

attributes   " 'My parts° had power to charm a sacred nun,   260
Who, disciplined, ay, dieted in grace,[8]
Believed her eyes when they t' assail begun,[9]
All vows and consecrations giving place.[10]
potent   O most potential° love! Vow, bond, nor space,
In thee hath neither sting, knot, nor confine,[11]   265
For thou art all, and all things else are thine.

" 'When thou impressest,[12] what are precepts worth
outdated / want to   Of stale° example? When thou wilt° inflame,
ineffectually   How coldly° those impediments [13] stand forth
Of wealth, of filial fear,[14] law, kindred, fame.   270
Love's arms are peace,[15] 'gainst rule, 'gainst sense,
     'gainst shame,
And sweetens, in the suff'ring pangs it bears,[16]
bitterness   The aloes° of all forces, shocks, and fears.

1 *bleeding groans*

   It was a common belief that a drop of blood was lost with each sigh.

2 *To leave the batt'ry that you make 'gainst mine*

   To cease the attack you make against my heart

3 *Lending soft audience to my sweet design*

   Responding favorably to my gentle wooing

4 *prefer and undertake my troth*

   Recommend and guarantee my promise

5 *levelled on*

   Set on; aimed at

6 *Each cheek a river running from a fount / With brinish current downward flowed apace*

   On each of his cheeks a river flowed from his eyes, with salty water rapidly running downward.

7 *glazed with crystal gate*

   Created a crystalline cover over

8 *the glowing roses / That flame through water which their hue encloses*

   The blushing cheeks that glow through the tears that cover their complexion

9 *father*

   (See line 71 and note)

10 *hell of witchcraft*

   A vast amount of bewitching charms

11 *But with the inundation of the eyes / What rocky heart to water will not wear?*

   But with a flood of tears, what stony heart would not erode?

12 *cleft effect*

   Ambiguous result

13 *Both fire from hence and chill extincture hath*

   Both fire and chill have extinction from (i.e., are extinguished by) the same source.

14 *lo, his passion, but an art of craft*

   Alas, his passionate speech was but trickery.

15 *guards and civil fears*

   Defenses and polite worries

16 *Appear to him, as he to me appears, / All melting*

   And appeared to him as he came to me, all dissolved in tears

17 *did him restore*

   Restored him to health

" 'Now all these hearts that do on mine depend,
languish   Feeling it break, with bleeding groans[1] they pine,°   275
in supplication   And suppliant° their sighs to you extend
To leave the batt'ry that you make 'gainst mine,[2]
Lending soft audience to my sweet design,[3]
trusting   And credent° soul to that strong-bonded oath
That shall prefer and undertake my troth.'[4]   280

lower   "This said, his wat'ry eyes he did dismount,°
Whose sights till then were levelled on[5] my face;
Each cheek a river running from a fount
With brinish current downward flowed apace.[6]
Oh, how the channel to the stream gave grace,   285
Which   Who° glazed with crystal gate[7] the glowing roses
That flame through water which their hue encloses.[8]

"O father,[9] what a hell of witchcraft[10] lies
individual   In the small orb of one particular° tear!
But with the inundation of the eyes   290
What rocky heart to water will not wear?[11]
What breast so cold that is not warmèd here?
O cleft effect![12] Cold modesty, hot wrath,
Both fire from hence and chill extincture hath.[13]

"For, lo, his passion, but an art of craft,[14]   295
dissolved   Even there resolved° my reason into tears;
took off   There my white stole of chastity I daffed,°
Shook off my sober guards and civil fears,[15]
Appear to him, as he to me appears,
All melting;[16] though our drops this difference bore: 300
His poisoned me, and mine did him restore.[17]

1   *all strange forms receives*

I.e., the *subtle matter* assumes
various guises.

2   *and he takes and leaves, / In either's aptness as it best deceives*

He takes or leaves whichever of
these forms works best for deception.

3   *speeches rank*

Offensive speech

4   *hail of his all-hurting aim*

Imagining his desire to indiscrimi-
nately injure as a *hail* (as in "a hail of
bullets") of malicious intention

5   *Showing fair nature is both kind and tame*

Revealing that an honest nature is
trusting and malleable

6   *veiled in them, did win whom he would
maim*

Disguised in his fair appearance
he won over those whom he would
harm.

7   *When he most burned in heart-wished
luxury, / He preached pure maid*

When he burned with lustful desire,
he preached virginity

8   *merely with the garment of a grace / The
naked and concealèd fiend he covered*

With only the appearance of beauty
or virtue, he covered up the naked
devil below.

9   *That th' unexperient gave the tempter
place*

So that those who were inexperi-
enced made room for the devil

10   *be so lovered*

Take him as her lover

11   *do question make / What I should do
again for such a sake*

Ask what I would do if I had another
such opportunity

12   *forced thunder from*

Contrived bombast that from

13   *sad breath*

Plaintive sigh

14   *all that borrowed motion seeming owed*

All his affected emotions that
seemed truly to be his own

15   *betray the fore-betrayed, / And new
pervert a reconcilèd maid*

Betray her who already had been
betrayed, and newly corrupt a
penitent maid

"In him a plenitude of subtle matter,
tricks; deceptions   Applied to cautels,° all strange forms receives,[1]
Of burning blushes, or of weeping water,
Or swooning paleness; and he takes and leaves,   305
In either's aptness as it best deceives,[2]
To blush at speeches rank,[3] to weep at woes,
events   Or to turn white and swoon at tragic shows.°

So that / line of fire   "That° not a heart which in his level° came
Could 'scape the hail of his all-hurting aim,[4]   310
Showing fair nature is both kind and tame;[5]
And, veiled in them, did win whom he would maim.[6]
Against the thing he sought he would exclaim:
When he most burned in heart-wished luxury,
He preached pure maid and praised cold chastity.[7]   315

"Thus merely with the garment of a grace
The naked and concealèd fiend he covered,[8]
That th' unexperient gave the tempter place,[9]
protecting angel   Which like a cherubin° above them hovered.
Who, young and simple, would not be so lovered?[10]   320
Ay me, I fell; and yet do question make
What I should do again for such a sake.[11]

infectious; corrupted   "Oh, that infected° moisture of his eye,
Oh, that false fire which in his cheek so glowed,
Oh, that forced thunder from[12] his heart did fly,   325
Oh, that sad breath[13] his spongy lungs bestowed,
Oh, all that borrowed motion seeming owed,[14]
Would yet again betray the fore-betrayed,
And new pervert a reconcilèd maid!'[15]

Longer Notes to Shakespeare's *Sonnets* and "A Lover's Complaint"

Sonnets

PAGE 31

Sonnets 1–17

Called the procreation sonnets, these first 17 sonnets derive from a widely copied and imitated epistle by Erasmus urging a young man of high rank to marry and beget children; according to its logic, the social order depends on the reproduction of lineage. For Shakespeare, it is particularly the youth's beauty that must be propagated, though his beauty is often affiliated with the nobility of his descent.

PAGE 69

Sonnet 20

Termed the "master-mistress" sonnet, this poem highlights the androgynous attractions of the beloved. The context activates a number of double entendres on male and female genitalia: *acquainted* (3) contains "quaint," slang for vulva, *thing* (12) is the male member, and *nothing* (12) the female lack of that member (and, of course, *pricked* in line 13). The ambiguity extends to the couplet in which the beloved's male anatomy both precludes sex with the male poet and allows for it. (For the latter possibility, compare Martial's Epigram XI.22.9–10: "Nature has divided the male: one part is made for girls, one for men.") Only this sonnet and Sonnet 87 consistently use feminine rhymes (made up of an extra unstressed final syllable); in verse of the period, feminine rhymes often occur in titillating contexts.

PAGE 273

Sonnet 122   *tables (1, 12)*
Also called a tablebook: a portable bound volume of blank pages in which the owner recorded memorabilia, often including verse. In Sonnet 77, the poet gives such a book to his friend; here the poet admits to having given away the one his friend had given to him. Hamlet makes use of his tables to inscribe a maxim just after the Ghost's departure (1.5.107-8).

PAGE 281

Sonnet 126 (   )/(   )
The two sets of empty parentheses appear in Q and draw attention to the sonnet's truncated form. They have been seen as graphic renderings of the symbols of mortality named or implied within the sonnet:

sickles, waning moons, an hourglass, marks in audit books, and open graves, though they may merely be a printer's anxious recognition that the sonnet has only twelve lines. In any case, the unusual sonnet, consisting of six couplets, is usually taken to mark the end of the sonnets addressed to a male friend. Often, however, the gender of the addressee is not specified, though there are no sonnets explicitly addressed to a female in sonnets 1 through 126 and none to a male in 127 to 154.

PAGE 299 AND 300

Sonnets 135 and 136   *Will*
This and the following sonnet play rampantly on Shakespeare's first name, repeating *Will* or *will* 20 times in a total of 28 lines. In Q, the word's ubiquity is heightened by its having been capitalized and italicized in 10 uses. *Will* also denotes sexual desire and

the organs of sexual desire: of the poet, of other men, and of the mistress. (It is, of course, also the auxiliary verb indicating futurity [136.5]) In both sonnets, Will equates his proper name with not only his lust but also that of his promiscuous mistress and her countless lovers.

PAGE 321

Sonnet 146   [   ]

In Q, the three words that end line one are repeated here. Editors have emended this obvious error with phrases of their own devising, for example: "Fool'd by" "Starv'd by," "Hemmed with," "Gull'd by," "Feeding these," "Seiged by," "Spoiled by," and "Pressed with." It is left blank here, as a reminder of the many uncertainties attending the sonnets.

PAGES 335 AND 337

Sonnets 153 and 154

Both sonnets originate in a much translated Greek epigram in which the attempt to douse Cupid's torch sets water aflame. Together they underscore the unquenchability of desire, as demonstrated by the previous 152 sonnets and confirmed by the ensuing "A Lover's Complaint."

A Lover's Complaint

PAGE 338

"A Lover's Complaint"

This poem belongs to a subgenre of female complaint poems and ballads, narrating in a female voice stories of women who have been undone by men. Several sonnet sequences printed before Shakespeare's conclude with such female complaints. The poem's vocabulary and syntax have been archaized by the poet, perhaps to distinguish it from the more courtly and urbane sonnets, and to conform with the poem's rural setting amidst hills and vales (1–2), along a riverbank (38), with cattle grazing near by (57). Shakespeare's authorship of this poem has frequently been questioned.

PAGE 339

1.3   *double voice*

The complaint first registers as an echo, as if the love story were reverberating from the preceding sonnets. The voice, however, is female, as recorded by an unidentified male narrator.

PAGE 343

1.71   *"Father,"*

A respectful form of address, with priestly overtones. From this point on, the narration is in the maiden's voice, though she extensively quotes her suitor in 15 stanzas (ll.177–280).

PAGE 353

1.209   *deep-brained sonnets*

Among the tokens with which the young man woos the maiden, are sonnets, and they, too, have been given to him by other women. Their recycling suggests their suitability for either sex. Like Shakespeare's sonnets, they are ungendered or can easily be regendered. In both manuscript and print from the 17th century, there is evidence that some of Shakespeare's sonnets from 1 to 126

were read as if addressed to a
woman, as they often still are
today.

SHAKE-SPEARES,
SONNETS.

FRom faireſt creatures we deſire increaſe,
   That thereby beauties *Roſe* might neuer die,
But as the riper ſhould by time deceaſe,
His tender heire might beare his memory:
But thou contracted to thine owne bright eyes,
Feed'ſt thy lights flame with ſelfe ſubſtantiall fewell,
Making a famine where aboundance lies,
Thy ſelfe thy foe, to thy ſweet ſelfe too cruell:
Thou that art now the worlds freſh ornament,
And only herauld to the gaudy ſpring,
Within thine owne bud burieſt thy content,
And tender chorle makſt waſt in niggarding:
   Pitty the world, or elſe this glutton be,
   To eate the worlds due, by the graue and thee.

2

VVHen fortie Winters ſhall beſeige thy brow,
   And digge deep trenches in thy beauties field,
Thy youthes proud liuery ſo gaz'd on now,
Wil be a totter'd weed of ſmal worth held:
Then being askt, where all thy beautie lies,
Where all the treaſure of thy luſty daies;
To ſay within thine owne deepe ſunken eyes,
Were an all-eating ſhame, and thriftleſſe praiſe.
How much more praiſe deſeru'd thy beauties vſe,
If thou couldſt anſwere this faire child of mine
Shall ſum my count, and make my old excuſe
Proouing his beautie by ſucceſſion thine.

B

This

Editing the *Sonnets* and "A Lover's Complaint"

by David Scott Kastan

n 1609 a book entitled *Shake-speares Sonnets* was published in London and advertised on its title page as "Neuer before Imprinted." That May the publisher, Thomas Thorpe, had announced his intention to publish the edition, registering the book with the Stationers' Company, paying six pence to preserve his copyright. The book was apparently in print by June, as Edward Allyn, the great contemporary actor, noted his purchase, for five pence, of "a book Shaksper sonnetts" on the back of a letter dated 19 June 1609. The thin volume contained 154 sonnets and a short narrative poem "A Lover's Complaint." Thirteen copies of it survive.

Versions of two of the sonnets (138 and 144) had been published in 1599 in a small collection of verse called *The Passionate Pilgrim*, and a number, perhaps the entire collection, had seemingly circulated in manuscript. In 1598, Francis Meres mentioned the circulation of Shakespeare's "sugared sonnets among his friends," but, though manuscript versions of twenty-five sonnets survive, none is in Shakespeare's hand and all of these can be dated after his death. The sonnets were reprinted in 1640, published by John Benson, who omitted some, ignored the 1609 order, combined a number of them to make single longer poems, and included in the edition material by other authors. Therefore the 1609 edition must be the source of any modern edition of the *Sonnets* as well as of "A Lover's Complaint," for which it is the only surviving text.

The 1609 Quarto is reasonably well printed; both the printer, George Eld, and the publisher Thomas Thorpe, were reputable members of the book trade and often worked together on literary projects, though it is not clear how they came into possession of the manuscript of the poem or what that manuscript represents. Was it in Shakespeare's hand? Did it represent his own ordering of the poems? We do not know for sure, although the scholarly consensus is that the manuscript, at least in part, was a copy made by a scribe, but which may well preserve the author's ordering of the poems. No greater certainty on this is possible. A modern edition, therefore, has little choice but to retain the order of the 1609 edition. The poems themselves are for the most part coherent as they appear, demanding only occasional emendation to make sense of obvious errors. The textual notes below record all substantive changes that this edition makes from the 1609 printing.

In general the editorial principles that underlie this Barnes & Noble edition are conservative; that is, changes of Q are generally confined to modernization. Spelling, capitalization, and italicization are for the most part modernized to conform to our own contemporary practices rather than those of the 1609 printing house. Neither spelling nor punctuation had yet been standardized. Words were spelled in various ways to indicate their proximate pronunciation, and punctuation, which was in general more a rhythmical pointer than predominately designed, as it is now, to clarify logical relations, was more idiosyncratic than it is today. In any case, as the compositors in the printing house, that is, the men who actually set the type, were under no obligation to follow either the spelling or the punctuation of their copy, it isn't clear that what appears in 1609 is any more than a house style that perhaps represents only what the compositors understood rather than what Shakespeare intended. And indeed as we know so little about the manuscript that they worked from, it is possible that that too in various ways misrepresented Shakespeare's characteristic spelling or punctuation habits. For most readers, then, there is little advantage in an edition that reproduces the spelling and punctuation of Q. It does not necessarily represent Shakespeare's preferences, and it makes reading difficult in a way Shakespeare could never have anticipated or desired.

A look at the facsimile of the first page of the *Sonnets* (page 368) and a comparison of what is there with what is printed here may allow the editorial process to become clear. Various things are immediately obvious. One is the spelling of Shakespeare with a hyphen, which some who don't believe that the actor from Stratford wrote the plays and poems attributed to William Shakespeare take as witty evidence that this should be recognized as a pseudonym, though the entry in the Stationer's register refers to the book as "SHAKESPEARES sonnettes," and unauthorized hyphenation of names is not uncommon and indeed is sometimes introduced in the printing house to prevent pieces of type whose edges might bang together in the printing process (as is possible with the capital E and S) from being damaged. As interesting is the comma following SHAKE-SPEARES, which itself shows the unreliability of punctuation and how misleading relying on it might be.

It is also worth noting that Sonnet 2 does not entirely fit on this page (and is, of course, continued on the next), unlike some early editions of Renaissance sonnets that print one sonnet per page. This is a decision made in the printing house, primarily to preserve paper, and there is no reason for a modern edition to follow the page breaks produced by this nonauthorial, material consideration.

But perhaps more interesting is the evidence of the different linguistic environment in which Shakespeare worked. Beyond the unfamiliar letterforms (for example the ligature (a single piece of type that joins two letters) "st" in "fairest" in line one of Sonnet 1 shows the long "s" also present in "desire" and "increase" at the end of the line, there is the "u" in neuer" in line 2 and the "v" beginning the word "use" in line 9 of Sonnet 2. In Shakespeare's time "u" and "v" were more or less interchangeable, "v" usually used for "u" at the beginning of a word and "u" for "v" in the middle (as also in "graue" in line 14 of Sonnet 1), though note also that "u" is merely "u" in words like "gaudy" in line 10 of Sonnet 1. Also there are the intrusive final "e"s that modern English has dropped, as in "heire" and "beare" in line 4 of Sonnet 1. There are archaic or idiosyncratic spellings, like "fewell" for the modern "fuel." There is no use here of the apostrophe to indicate possession, so "beauties" in line 2 of Sonnet 1 or line 2 of Sonnet 2 is what we would write as "beauty's," and "worlds" in line 14 of Sonnet 1 would be "world's."

All of these are easily and unproblematically modernized. Sometimes it is harder: does "fild" (e.g., in line 3 of Sonnet 63) mean "filled" or "filed," both of which make sense in context? Nonetheless, modern spelling is introduced along with modern punctuation habits. Q's version of lines 9–12 in Sonnet 2 reads:

> How much more praise deseru'd thy beauties vse,
> If though couldst answere this faire child of mine
> Shall sum my count, and make my old excuse
> Proouing his beautie by succession thine.

Modernized this reads:

> How much more praise deserved thy beauty's use
> If thou couldst answer, "This fair child of mine
> Shall sum my count and make my old excuse,"
> Proving his beauty by succession thine.

No doubt there is some loss in the modernization. Intelligibility and consistency are gained at the expense of expressive detail. But normalizing the spelling, letterforms, and punctuation allows the poems to be read by modern readers with far greater ease than the original, and essentially as it was intended to be understood. We lose the archaic feel of the text in exchange for clarity of meaning. Old spellings throughout this edition are consistently modernized, but old forms of words are retained (thus "art," meaning "are," in line 9 of Sonnet 1 is kept, but "totter'd" in line 4 of Sonnet 2 is changed in this edition to "tattered"—and the metrical cue of Q's apostrophe that this is not supposed to be pronounced totterèd, or tatterèd, is acknowledged in that the unsounded participle is the normal modern pronunciation, where sounded participles appear in this edition with accented "è"s).

If in this editorial process we lose the historical feel of the text Shakespeare's contemporaries read, it is important to remember that Shakespeare's contemporaries would not have thought the poems they read on the page in any way archaic or quaint, as these details make them for a reader today. They text of Q would have seemed to them as modern as this one does to us. Modern readers, however, cannot help but be distracted by the different conventions they encounter on the page of an early text. While it is indeed of interest to see how orthography and typography have changed over time, these changes are not primary concerns of most readers of this edition. What little, then, is lost in a careful modernization of the text of *Sonnets* and "A Lover's Complaint" is more than made for by the removal of the artificial obstacle of unfamiliar spelling forms and punctuation habits, which Shakespeare never could have intended as interpretive difficulties for his readers.

Textual Notes:

The list below records all substantive departures in this edition from the 1609 quarto (Q) of *Sonnets* and "A Lover's Complaint." It does not record modernizations of spelling and punctuation, normalization of the use of capitals, or corrections of obvious typographical errors. The adopted reading in this edition is given below with sonnet and line number (or in the case of "A Lover's Complaint," only the line number) all in boldface and followed by the reading in roman as it appears in Q.

Sonnets:

2.14 cold could; **12.4 all** or; **13.7 Yourself** You selfe; **15.8 wear** were; **19.3 jaws** yawes; **23.14 with** wit; **23.14 wit** wiht; **25.9 might** worth; **26.12 thy** their; **27.10 thy** their; **34.12 cross** losse; **35.8 thy . . . thy** their . . . their; **37.7 thy** their; **40.7 thyself** this selfe; **43.11 thy** their; **44.13 naught** naughts; **45.9 life's** lives; **45.12 thy** their; **46.3,8,13,14 thy** their; **46.9 'cide** side; **47.11 no** nor; **50.6 dully** duly; **51.10 perfect'st** pefects; **54.14 my** by; **55.1 monuments** monument; **56.13 Or** As; **69.3 due** end; **69.5 Thy** Their; **70.6 thy** their; **76.7 tell** fel; **77.1 wear** were; **77.10 blanks** blacks; **90.11 shall** stall; **91.9 better** bitter; **99.5 dyed** died; **99.9 One** Our; **106.12 skill** still; **110.9 save** haue; **111.1 with** wish; **112.8 o'erchanges** or changes; **113.6 latch** lack; **113.14 mine eye** mine; **126.8 minutes** mynuit; **128.11, 14 thy** their; **129.9 Mad** Made; **129.11 proved, a** proud and; **144.6 side** sight; **144.9 fiend** finde; **146.2 [**] My sinfull earth

"A Lover's Complaint":

14 lattice lettice; **37 beaded** bedded; **95 wear** were; **103 breathe** breath; **118 Came** Can; **182 woo** vow; **241 Planing** Playing; **251 immured** enur'd; **252 procured** procure; **260 nun** Sunne; **293 O** Or; **305 swooning** sounding; **308 swoon** sound

For Further Reading

Booth, Stephen, ed. *Shakespeare's Sonnets*. New Haven, CT: Yale University Press, 1977. Runs a modern edition against a facsimile of the 1609 edition, followed by 400 pages of analytic commentary, dazzlingly attentive to the complex workings of language.

Burrow, Colin, ed. *Complete Sonnets and Poems*. Oxford: Oxford University Press, 2002). A magnificent scholarly edition, accessible and lively, with comprehensive introductions to both the sonnets and "A Lover's Complaint."

Cheney, Patrick, ed. *The Cambridge Companion to Shakespeare's Poetry*. Cambridge: Cambridge University Press, 2007). A number of the essays explore the theatricality of the sonnets, as well as the role of poetry in the plays.

Edmondson, Paul and Wells, Stanley. *Shakespeare's Sonnets*. Oxford Shakespeare Topics. Oxford: Oxford University Press, 2004. A fresh and widely informed overview of key issues, with sections on the various transformations of the sonnets into music, poetry, novels, theater, and film.

Fineman, Joel. *Shakespeare's Perjured Eye: The Invention of Poetic Subjectivity in the Sonnets*. Berkeley: University of California Press, 1986. A monumental (and monumentally challenging) analysis that interrelates the poetic and the psychoanalytic in crediting the sonnets with inventing a genuinely modern "I."

Freinkel, Lisa. *Reading Shakespeare's Will: The Theology of Figure from Augustine to the Sonnets*. New York: Columbia University Press, 2002. A probing reading of the sonnets in terms of the theological tradition from Augustine through to the Reformation.

Magnusson, Lynne. *Shakespeare and Social Dialogue: Dramatic Language and Elizabethan Letters*. Cambridge: Cambridge University Press, 1999. Contains an illuminating analysis of how class differentials inflect the language and emotion of the sonnets.

Pequigney, Joseph. *Such Is My Love: A Study of Shakespeare's Sonnets*. Chicago: Chicago University Press, 1985. An autobiographical reading, supported by historical materials, arguing for Shakespeare's passion for a young man.

Schalkwyk, David. *Speech and Performance in Shakespeare's Sonnets and Plays*. Cambridge: Cambridge University Press, 2002. A philosophically inflected study of the sonnets as speech acts with performative features and consequences.

Schiffer, James, ed. *Shakespeare's Sonnets: Critical Essays*. New York: Garland Publishing, 1999. A collection of critical essays representing the best work from a decade of innovative criticism on the sonnets.

Schoenfeldt, Michael, ed. *A Companion to Shakespeare's Sonnets*. Malden, MA: Blackwell, 2007. Twenty-five recent essays, some focused on their aesthetic features, others on their sociopolitical contexts, and some combining the two.

Sharon-Zisser, *Critical Essays on Shakespeare's "A Lover's Complaint": Suffering Ecstasy.* Aldershot, Burlington, VT: Ashgate, 2006. The first collection of essays on "A Complaint," exploring its various contexts and attempting to validate its admission to the Shakespearean canon.

Smith, Bruce. *Homosexual Desire in Shakespeare's England: A Cultural Poetics.* Chicago: University of Chicago Press, 1991. A lucid and sophisticated analysis of love between men in Shakespeare's time in which the sonnets figure centrally.

Vendler, Helen. *The Art of Shakespeare's Sonnets.* Cambridge, MA: Harvard University Press, Belknap Press, 1997. Detailed commentaries alongside each sonnet by one of the most gifted and accomplished readers of poetry of our time.

Oscar Wilde, *The Portrait of Mr W.H.,* ed. Vyvyan Holland. London: Methuen, 1958. First published in 1889, a brilliant interweaving of criticism, fiction, and fantasy that brings those two enigmatic initials to life.